▲ ▲ ▲
HEAD
TO
TOE

by
Hélène Rush

30 Original Designs for
Hats, Mittens, and Other Accessories

▲ ▲ ▲

DOWN EAST BOOKS / CAMDEN, MAINE

Book design by Janet Patterson
Typography by Typeworks, Belfast, Me.
Color separations by Four Colour Imports, Louisville, Ky.
Printed and bound at Capital City Press, Inc., Montpelier, Vt.

9 8 7 6 5 4 3 2

Down East Books
P.O. Box 679, Camden, ME 04843

HEAD
TO
TOE

Contents

Preface

It is snowing outside; the skies are gray and everything is covered with white. In the snowbank a patch of color emerges: rosy cheeks, bright eyes, and a wonderful cap with cheery motifs. What better way to brighten up these cold days than to work up a trunkful of accessories for the whole family!

Come Christmas time, hang those special stockings from the fireplace mantel, to be filled with wonderful memories year after year. Cuddle up under a wooly afghan while dreaming of puffins, pine trees, and sailboats. And keep your toes warm in a pair of slippers guaranteed to be the envy of all.

This third book of "woolies" featuring Maine motifs includes a collection of accessories to knit for you and your loved ones. As a special gift or just to show you care, they are sure to be enjoyed by all.

Acknowledgments

I would like to thank the people at Harrisville Designs, especially Leslie Voiers, for being so generous with the materials furnished for all the projects in this book. Anyone who wishes to exactly duplicate the accessories shown here can purchase wool through Harrisville's mail-order service.

A special thanks is extended to the knitters, without whom I would still be knitting for this book to this day. Susan Wills, Letty McDonough, and Susan Worthing, you did a great job!

And finally, to my family, who constantly put up with my knitting ''stuff'' all over the house, and who complain very little about Mom being so busy—a warm hug to you all.

Introduction

In this book you will find a collection of thirty patterns ranging from mittens and hats to Christmas stockings, and an afghan and pillow set. Most styles reflect Maine themes, while others have varied inspirations. All present a colorful medley of accessories for your family and home.

Material Selection

I have been fortunate to have been provided by Harrisville Designs with their wide palette of wools. The colors are brilliant and are offered in sixty heathery tones and twenty-four tweeds. At times their wide selection of marvelous hues made my choices difficult! Their color card reads ''Color is our business''—believe it!

Of course, your favorite yarn shop is sure to offer a wide variety of other yarns that could be good substitutes for the ones shown here. Don't be afraid to try other yarns or colors, but do be sure to match the gauge!

Because most of the items included in this collection are obviously made to be worn in winter, I only used 100% wool for all projects. For all but a few of the larger items, one skein of each color was needed. I have used two weights of yarn: worsted and sport, with gauges of 5 stitches and 7 stitches per inch, respectively.

I know that some knitters will substitute acrylic yarn for wool. Sometimes it is for the price, although two or three skeins of wool for a hat and mittens set will not cost much more. Sometimes it is for the easy-care qualities of acrylic; however, wool can be washed in the delicate cycle of your machine and it will not take much time to air dry a hat or mittens. Besides, how often every winter does anyone wash mittens and hats? And then sometimes it is because of complaints about wool feeling itchy close to the skin. I have solved that problem for hats by inserting a four- to five-inch lining of lightweight knit fabric inside the brim. Whatever you decide, I

still say wool is much warmer than any synthetic fibers!

Gauge

For those of you who already have copies of my previous books, you know by now how much emphasis I put on working with the correct gauge. I *know* how time consuming it is to work a 4-inch by 4-inch swatch when all you are planning to knit is a teeny little hat. I guess if you have children in assorted sizes, the hat is bound to fit someone in the family. If not, you can always donate it to a rummage sale—or maybe it could be used as a potholder. Then again, maybe that color of yarn was going to match perfectly with your new parka, and now who knows how cold your ears are going to be . . .

Well, fret no more. Pick up those needles and work a four-inch by four-inch swatch to be sure all is going to fit. Begin by using the suggested needle size in the pattern, even if you are going to use Harrisville Designs wools. If the gauge is listed at 5 stitches per inch, cast on 20 stitches, if it is listed at 7 stitches per inch, cast on 28 stitches. Work in stockinette stitch (unless otherwise indicated) for 4 inches. Remove the stitches from the needle, lay the swatch on a flat surface, and measure across. If the swatch is too big, start all over again with needles one size smaller; if it is too small, try one size larger. Keep going until you match the gauge listed perfectly. Indicate somewhere which size needles you ended up using with what type of yarn so you will save time on future projects.

If you decide to use a different yarn than the Harrisville Designs choices shown here, first make sure the suggested gauge listed on the yarn's skein band falls in the 4.5 to 5.5 stitches per inch range (to substitute for patterns listing a 5 sts per inch gauge), or in the 6.5 to 7.5 per inch range (for patterns listing a 7 sts per inch gauge). Then, begin your ''quest for gauge'' by using the recommended needle size on the skein band of your substitute yarn and work from there until you get it right.

What Size to Make

One thing I found out while working on this book is that people's hands come in a lot more sizes than I would have ever imagined. Some people need extra wide, very short mittens, while others have pianists' hands. So I have tried to write average-sized patterns and give a few guidelines to help you decide which size to make. Some patterns are written for both children's and adult's sizes, while others only list one or the other. Both glove patterns included in this book are written in one size only, leaving it up to you to adjust hand and finger lengths accordingly. Sock patterns also will need some adjustments when it comes to length. Ideally, you will be able to take some basic measurements from the person for whom you are knitting and thus ensure a close-fitting sock.

Another thing I found out while working on this book is that although your head may measure 21 inches, if you want the hat to stay on, you need to make it at least one inch smaller. The patterns here range from 17 to 20 inches in diameter. You can always measure an old hat that fits just right and then select the corresponding pattern size.

Supply Sources

Harrisville Designs
Harrisville, NH 03450
603-827-3332

Retails knitting and weaving yarns, and a complete line of looms and weaving accessories. Source of the specific yarns shown in this book.

Sportsman Manufacturing Company
111 Commercial Street
Berlin, WI 54923
414-361-2666

Retails shearling leather soles for slippers.

Working with Harrisville Designs Wools

Although Harrisville Designs primarily spins yarns for handweaving, more and more knitters are discovering that their wool is perfectly suited for knitwear projects too. I have had the pleasure of working with their yarns on previous occasions and was very happy when they agreed to supply me with materials for this book. These patterns use either the Two Ply (100-gram skeins, 220 yards) or Shetland Style (100-gram skeins, 440 yards).

Because of the special way that they spin their wool, it may at first feel scratchy to some people. Washing the wool—either in the skein or as a completed garment—will remedy that problem. I have gone through both processes, following the steps listed below.

Washing in the skein: Untwist the skein and then, using strands of scrap yarn, loosely tie it in eight different places around the circumference. Using warm water and the ''delicate'' setting fill your washing machine with a minimum amount of water, squirt in a small quantity of dishwashing liquid, then immerse the yarn skeins. Agitate slowly for about one minute, drain the water and allow the machine to spin until rinse cycle begins. Once cool water is filled for rinse cycle, allow the machine to agitate for about one minute again, then advance the cycle to the point where the machine will drain the rinse water and do the final spin cycle.

Washing by hand (in the skein) is also possible, though it's much more work than the machine-wash method. Open skein and tie in one additional place with scrap yarn. In lukewarm water, with mild soap, knead the skein as you would bread for 5 to 10 minutes or until the desired amount of fluffiness is obtained. (But note that too much or too-vigorous kneading will cause wool to felt.) Rinse twice in tepid water. Gently squeeze out excess water and wrap skein in towel to absorb water, or spin dry in washing machine as described above.

Hang the skeins outside to dry, if possible, and not in direct sunlight. Allow the yarn to dry thoroughly before winding into balls. The yarn will now be soft and fluffy and will have done its shrinking. You may need to adjust the suggested needle sizes if you opt to use this washing method since the yarn will have thickened somewhat.

Washing after knitting: Follow the same steps as for washing in the skein, except use cold water instead of warm. Once garments are out of the machine, lay them flat to dry on a towel. When almost dry, lightly press with a warm iron and damp cloth, being careful not to press ribbed area and keeping garment from being pulled out of shape.

List of Abbreviations

Several common knitting abbreviations are used in this book; here is a list for reference:

St, sts: Stitch, stitches
K: Knit
P: Purl
Yo: Yarn over needle
K2 tog, p2 tog: Knit or purl 2 stitches together.
Ssk (left decrease): Insert needle in front of first stitch, then in back of next stitch and knit these 2 stitches together.
Rep: Repeat
Inc: Increase, increasing
Dec: Decrease, decreasing
Sl: Slip
Psso: Pass slipped stitch over
St st: Stockinette stitch

Special Techniques

The key to a perfect knitted item lies in the finishing. Pay special attention to the knitted seam and outside seam methods illustrated here. Done correctly, these finishing touches are sure to enhance any projects you have spent all those patient hours working on.

French Knots

Using a yarn needle, pull yarn through fabric where you want the knot to be, then wrap the yarn around the needle twice.

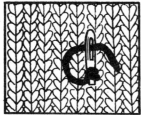

Reinsert needle right next to where it first came out. Pull yarn through the fabric, keeping the knot on the right side.

Duplicate Stitch

Draw the yarn needle through the fabric at the base of the stitch you want to cover. Then insert the needle from left to right behind the base of the stitch directly above this stitch. Draw the yarn through.

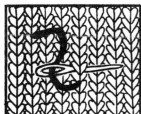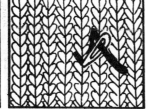

Reinsert the needle at base of the stitch to be covered.

Knitted Seam Method

Place shoulder stitches back onto needles from stitch holders. Hold needles together with right sides of fabric touching each other. Then, using a third needle (same size as used for the main part of sweater), insert it through the first stitch of both needles and knit together.

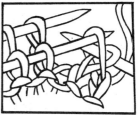

Repeat for next stitch on both needles. Then pass first stitch on right needle over second one to bind it off. Repeat procedure until all stitches are bound off.

Weaving

This method can be used for any unbound edges where the same number of sts must be joined. It is also called grafting or kitchener stitch.

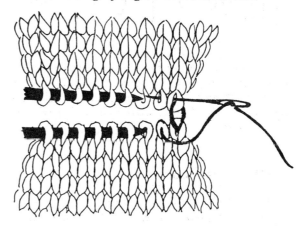

Insert threaded yarn needle purlwise (i.e., from back to front) through first stitch of front knit-

ting needle, and through first stitch of back knitting needle; re-insert needle knitwise (from front to back) through first stitch of front needle, then purlwise through second stitch of front needle. *Insert needle knitwise on stitch on back needle where thread emerges, purlwise through next stitch on needle. Insert needle knitwise through stitch on front needle where thread emerges, purlwise through next stitch on needle. Continue in this manner from * for rest of stitches, following illustration.

Try to keep the yarn tension of the weaving equal to that of the knitted pieces so that the joining loops are the same size as the rest of the stitches.

Outside Seam Method

With right side facing, working in half a stitch as illustrated (some people prefer working with a whole stitch on each side), insert needle in stitch under two rows on first side, then under two rows on second side. Repeat this side to side motion all the way to end of seam, pulling somewhat tightly on thread but keeping seam elastic.

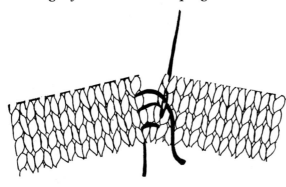

This seam method is most useful for joining pieces with color patterns. By working on the outside of the garment, you can control your stitch placement and obtain a perfect pattern match, thus making a seam practically impossible to detect.

Making a Pompom

Cut two circles of sturdy cardboard the desired diameter of the pompom, plus one inch. Cut a one-inch hole in the center of both pieces. Holding the two doughnut-shaped cardboard forms

together, cut a slit from outside edge to center hole. The slit should be wide enough to accommodate several thicknesses of yarn.

Continue holding the two forms together as you wrap yarn around the entire cardboard ring until it is quite full. Work with several strands of yarn at a time (in your selected color scheme) and wrap by passing the strands through the slit opening as you wind it around and around the ring.

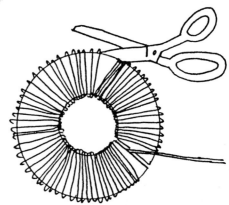

Cut the yarn strands along the entire outer edge of the ring, as illustrated. Without removing the cardboard forms, tie the pompom firmly around the middle with another length of yarn, sliding the tie down between the pieces of cardboard. Now remove the forms. Trim the pompom so it will be nice and round.

Buttonhole Stitch

Insert needle about ¼ inch from edge of buttonhole, and take out through buttonhole while holding thread under needle. Repeat around buttonhole.

Clockwise from upper left:
Child's Bunny Hat (p. 54),
Flock of Sheep Hat (p. 52),
Country Geese Hat (p. 50),
Summer Cottage Hat (p. 56).

Clockwise from upper right:
Square Deer Hat (p. 38), Deer
Mittens (p.40), Long Deer Hat
(p. 36), Deer Scarf (p. 42),
Child's Deer Vest (p. 44).

PHOTOGRAPHS BY JOE DEVENNEY

*Top: Child's Blueberry
Hat (p. 22), Adult's
Blueberry Hat (p. 25).
Bottom: Adult's
Blueberry Gloves
(p. 24), Child's
Blueberry Mittens
(p. 26).*

*Left: Chickadee Hat
(p. 47) and Mittens
(p. 48). Right: Child's
Pine Tree Hat (p. 34),
Socks (p. 32), and
Mittens (p. 33).*

*Crayon Kids Pullover (p. 58),
Hat (p. 60), and Mittens
(p. 62).*

*Clockwise from upper right:
Leather-Soled Slippers (p. 67),
Knitted-Sole Slippers (p. 68),
Norwegian Christmas
Stocking (p. 65), Pine Tree
Christmas Stocking (p. 63).*

Adult's Pine Tree Gloves (p. 27),
Socks (p. 30), and Hat (p. 28).

State of Maine Pillow (p. 72)
and Afghan (p. 70).

The Patterns

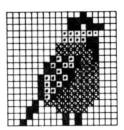

Child's Blueberry Hat

SIZES: 17 ½ (18 ½ –19) inches

MATERIALS: One 100-gram (220-yard) skein each Harrisville Two-Ply Tweed color Snowflake (A), color Purple (B) and color Dawn Mist (C). One pair each sizes 6 and 7 needles, or size needed to obtain correct gauge. One tapestry needle.

GAUGE: In pattern stitch with larger needles, 5 sts = 1 inch; in stockinette stitch with smaller needles, 5 sts = 1 inch.

PATTERN STITCH
Row 1: *(K1, yo, k1) in one stitch, p3; rep from *.

Row 2: *P3 tog, k3; rep from *.

Row 3: *P3, (k1, yo, k1) in next stitch; rep from *.

Row 4: *K3, p3 tog; rep from *.
Repeat these 4 rows for pattern stitch.

BRIM: With larger needles and color A, cast on 87 (91–95) sts. Change to smaller needles in row 1: P1, *k1, p1. Row 2: K1, *p1, k1. Work as established for 10 more rows. Next row with color B, K1, *yo, k2 tog; rep from *. Purl back with color B. Then, with color A in stockinette stitch, work 2 rows even, work next 8 rows following chart, work 2 rows even with color A. Then, with larger size needles, work 2 rows with color B, inc 1 st in first row, to make 88 (92–96) sts.

PATTERN STITCH BAND: Begin working pattern stitch with color A. At 4 ½ (5–5 ½) inches from eyelet row, begin shaping top.

TOP: Working in stockinette stitch with color B, dec 0 (4–8) sts evenly in first row, then purl back—88 sts. Row 1: K9, k2 tog across—80 sts. Row 2 and all wrong-side rows: Purl. Row 3: K8, k2 tog across—72 sts. Continue in this manner, decreasing evenly across as established, until 8 sts remain. Next right-side row, k2 tog across—4 sts. Cut yarn, leaving an eighteen-inch tail. With tapestry needle, weave tail through the 4 remaining sts and draw tightly to close opening.

FINISHING: Work blueberries in French knots (see Special Techniques) following placement on chart. Sew back seam. Fold ribbed cuff to inside on eyelet row (this will form a scalloped edge) and stitch cuff in place, working with loose tension so the cuff will be stretchy.

CHILD'S BLUEBERRY HAT CHART

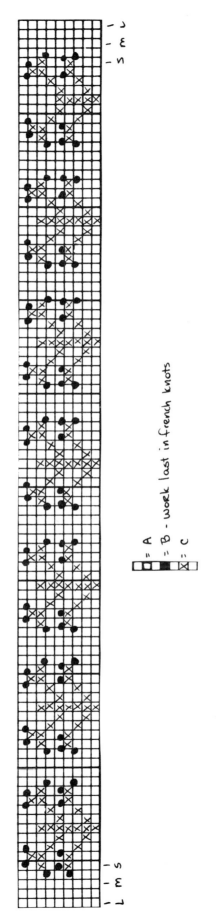

= A

= B - work last in french knots

= C

Blueberry Gloves

SIZES: This one pattern will fit sizes 6½, 7 and 7½. Individual finger-length adjustments can be made easily.

MATERIALS: One 100-gram (220-yard) skein each Harrisville Two-Ply Tweed color Snowflake (A), color Purple (B), and color Dawn Mist (C). One set size 6 double-pointed needles, or size needed to obtain correct gauge. Two markers. One tapestry needle.

GAUGE: In stockinette stitch, 5 sts = 1 inch.

LEFT GLOVE: With color B, cast on 52 sts. Working around, p1 row with color B, then k 2 rows with color C. Continue knitting every row with color A for next 14 rows. *At the same time,* beginning on 8th row, work chart for next 8 rows, work even with color A for 2 rows, dec 18 sts evenly in last row—34 sts. With color A, work in k1, p1 rib for 4 rows, then knit even for 1 inch, marking end of round.

THUMB GORE: Round 1: K 16, place marker on needle, inc 1 st in each of next 2 sts by knitting in the front and back of each st, place marker on needle, k 16. Round 2: Knit. Round 3: K to 1st marker, sl marker, inc in next st, k to 1 st before next marker, inc 1 st, sl marker, work to end of row. Repeat rounds 2 and 3 three more times to give 12 sts between markers. Next round, knit to 1st marker, remove marker, sl next 12 sts on holder for thumb, remove marker, cast on 2 sts, work to end of row—34 sts. Work even on these sts for 2 inches.

INDEX FINGER: K 12, leave on holder for palm, k next 10 sts, cast on 2 sts and leave remaining sts on holder for back of hand. Work around on these 12 sts for index finger until 2½ inches long, or desired length. Next row, k2 tog across

—6 sts. Cut yarn, leaving a 6-inch tail. With tapestry needle, weave this tail through remaining sts and draw tightly. Secure end to inside.

MIDDLE FINGER: Sl next 4 sts from back of hand holder to one needle and slip corresponding 4 sts from palm holder onto another needle. Working around, dividing sts evenly among 3 needles, pick up and k 2 sts on base of previous finger between back of hand and palm, k 4 sts, cast on 2 sts, k 4 sts. Work around on these 12 sts until finger is 2¾ inches long, or desired length. Complete as for first finger.

RING FINGER: Work as for middle finger for 2½ inches, or desired length.

LITTLE FINGER: Work as for other fingers on remaining 8 sts, but pick up 3 sts at base of previous finger and do not cast on sts on other side—11 sts. When 2¼ inches long, or desired length, complete as for first finger.

THUMB: Sl sts from thumb holder onto 3 needles, picking up 2 sts above the 2 cast-on sts from thumb gore to make 14 sts. Work around until 2½ inches long, or desired length. Complete as for first finger.

RIGHT GLOVE: Work as for left glove.

FINISHING: With tapestry needle and color B, work blueberries in French knots (see Special Techniques), positioning as on chart. Weave in all ends.

BLUEBERRY GLOVES CHART

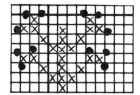

☐ = A

■ = B - work last in french knots

☒ = C

Adult's Blueberry Hat

SIZE: One size fits all.

MATERIALS: One 100-gram (220-yard) skein each Harrisville Two-Ply Tweed color Snowflake (A), color Purple (B), and color Dawn Mist (C). One 16-inch size 6 circular needle and one set size 6 double-pointed needles, or size needed to obtain correct gauge. One tapestry needle.

GAUGE: In stockinette stitch, 5 sts = 1 inch.

BRIM: With color B and using the circular needle, cast on 98 sts. Work around in k1, p1 rib for 2 rows with color B, then with color C until 1 inch from beginning. Then, with color A, begin shaping brim as follows: Row 1: *K13, inc in next st by working in front and back of stitch.* Repeat * to * 6 more times, to yield 105 sts. Row 2: Knit. Row 3: *K14, inc in next st.* Repeat * to * 6 times more, to yield 112 sts. Continue working increases every other row as established until you have 133 sts on needle. Then, work 3 rows of Chart 1. Work even until 4½ inches from beginning.

TOP SHAPING: Row 1: *K17, k2 tog* 7 times, to give 126 sts. Row 2: Knit. Row 3: *K16, k2 tog* 7 times, to give 119 sts. Continue decreasing in this manner every other row until you have 77 sts left, then work decreases every row until 7 sts remain, changing to double-pointed needles when necessary. Cut yarn, weave the end through remaining sts, and draw tightly to close opening.

FINISHING: Following Chart 2, work blueberry bushes in duplicate stitch in each of the 7 wedge-shaped areas of the hat, starting the motifs on third row above Chart 1. Then work blueberries in French knots following placement on chart. (See Special Techniques for instructions on duplicate stitch and French knots.)

ADULT'S BLUEBERRY HAT CHARTS

Chart 1

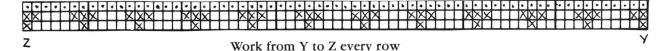

Z

Work from Y to Z every row

Y

Chart 2

☐ - A

■ - B - work last in french knots

☒ - C

Blueberry Mittens

SIZES: Children's sizes Small (Medium–Large)

MATERIALS: One 100-gram (220-yard) skein each Harrisville Two-Ply Tweed color Snowflake (A), color Purple (B), and color Dawn Mist (C). One pair each sizes 5 and 6 needles, or size needed to obtain correct gauge. One tapestry needle.

GAUGE: In stockinette stitch with size 5 needles, 5 sts = 1 inch.

CUFF: With larger needles and color C, cast on 39 (41–43) sts. In stockinette stitch, work 2 rows color B, 2 rows color A, then work following chart for 8 rows. Work 2 rows color A, dec 12 (10–10) sts evenly in last row, to leave 27 (31–33) sts. Then, with smaller needles and color A, work in ribs as follows: Row 1: K1, *p1, k1. Row 2: P1, *k1, p1. Repeat these 2 rows for 1 inch. Next, with larger needles, color A work in stockinette stitch for ¾ (1–1¼) inches. Then begin shaping thumb gore.

THUMB GORE: Row 1 (right side): Inc in first stitch by knitting in front and back of st, knit to last 2 sts, inc in next st, k1. Row 2 and all wrong-side rows: Purl. Row 3: K1, inc in next st, knit to last 3 sts, inc in next st, k2. Row 5: K2, inc in next st, knit to last 4 sts, inc in next st, k3. Continue in this manner until you have 39 (45–49) sts. Next row, wrong-side facing, purl 6 (7–8) sts and leave on holder, purl to last 6 (7–8) sts and turn, leaving these remaining sts on holder.

HAND: Work on remaining 27 (31–33) sts until 3¾ (4¾–5¾) inches from ribbing, or desired length. Dec 1 st in center of last row and place marker at halfway point—26 (30–32) sts.

SHAPE TOP: Row 1: Right side facing, with color B, k2 tog, k to 2 sts before marker, ssk, slip marker, k2 tog, work to last 2 sts, ssk—22 (26–28) sts. Row 2: Purl back. Repeat these 2 rows 2 more times, to leave 14 (18–20) sts. Break yarn. With tapestry needle, weave end shut and sew together the side of mitten up to thumb stitch holders (see Special Techniques, Outside Seam method).

THUMB: With larger needles and color B, k across sts from first holder, then across sts from second holder—12 (14–16) sts. Work back and forth in stockinette stitch for ¾ (1–1¼) inch. Row 1 (right side facing): K2 tog across, to leave 6 (7–8) sts. Row 2: P 0 (1–0), p2 tog across to end of row—3 (4–4) sts. With tapestry needle, weave through remaining sts and close end.

FINISHING: With tapestry needle and color B, work blueberries in French knots following placement on chart. Sew side seam on thumb and to end of cuff.

= A

= B - work last in french knots

X = C

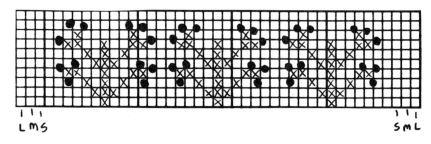

LMS

SML

Adult's Pine Tree Gloves

SIZES: This one pattern will fit sizes 6½, 7, and 7½. Individual finger-length adjustments can be made easily.

MATERIALS: One 100-gram (220-yard) skein Harrisville Two-Ply Tweed color Heath (A), one 100-gram (220-yard) skein each Harrisville Two-Ply no. 7 Sandalwood (B) and no. 31 Evergreen (C). One set size 6 double-pointed needles, or size needed to obtain correct gauge. Two markers. One tapestry needle.

GAUGE: In stockinette stitch, 5 sts = 1 inch.

LEFT GLOVE: With color C, cast on 30 sts loosely. Work around in k1, p1 rib for 2 rows, then continue in rib with color B until cuff is 2½ inches long. Knit next row with color B, inc 5 st in row to give 35 sts. Knit next 6 rows following Chart 1, marking end of round. Work 1 more row with Color B.

THUMB GORE: Work with color A. Round 1: K 16, place marker on needle, inc 1 st in each of next 2 sts, place marker on needle, k 17. Round 2: Knit. Round 3: K to first marker, sl marker, inc in next st, k to 1 st before next marker, inc 1 st, sl marker, work to end of row. Repeat rounds 2 and 3 three more times, to give 12 sts between markers. Next round, knit to first marker, remove marker, sl next 12 sts on holder for thumb, remove marker, cast on 1 st, work to end of row —34 sts. Work even on these sts for 2 inches.

INDEX FINGER: K 12, leave on holder for palm, k next 10 sts, cast on 2 sts, and leave remaining sts on holder for back of hand. Work

around on these 12 sts for index finger until 1½ inches long, or desired length. Work with color B for 1 inch more, to end of finger. Next row, k2 tog across, leaving 6 sts. Cut yarn, leaving a 6-inch tail. With tapestry needle, weave this tail through remaining sts and draw tightly. Secure end to inside.

MIDDLE FINGER: Sl next 4 sts from back of hand holder onto one needle, and slip corresponding 4 sts from palm holder onto another needle. Work around, dividing sts evenly on 3 needles: pick up and k 2 sts on base of previous finger between back of hand and palm, k 4 sts, cast on 2 sts, k 4 sts. Work on these 12 sts until finger is 1¾ inches long, or desired length. Work with color B for 1 inch more and then complete as for first finger.

RING FINGER: Work as for middle finger for 2½ inches total length (or desired size).

LITTLE FINGER: Work as for other fingers on remaining 8 sts but pick up 3 sts at base of previous finger and do not cast on sts on other side —11 sts. When 1¼ inches long, or desired length, work with color B for 1 inch more. Complete as for first finger.

THUMB: Sl sts from thumb holder on 3 needles, picking up 2 sts above the cast-on st of thumb gore, for a total of 14 sts. Work around until 1½ inches long, or desired length. Work with color B for 1 inch more. Complete as for first finger.

RIGHT GLOVE: Work as for left glove.

FINISHING: With tapestry needle and color C, work one pine tree motif in duplicate stitch (see Special Techniques), following Chart 2 and centering motif on back of glove. Weave in all ends.

Chart 1   Chart 2

☐ = A
• = B
☒ = C

Pine Tree Hat

SIZES: 18 (19–20) inches in circumference.

MATERIALS: One 100-gram (220-yard) skein Harrisville Two-Ply Tweed color Heath (A), one 100-gram (220-yard) skein each Harrisville Two-Ply no. 31 Evergreen (B) and no. 7 Sandalwood (C). One pair each sizes 5 and 6 needles, or size needed to obtain correct gauge.

GAUGE: In stockinette stitch with larger needles, 5 sts = 1 inch.

BRIM: With smaller needles and color C, cast on 91 (95–99) sts. Row 1: K1, *p1, k1. Row 2: P1, *k1, p1. Repeat for 2 more rows. Then, in stockinette stitch, work 2 rows with color C, work Chart 1 (6 rows), and then 2 rows with color C. Next, work in k1, p1 rib, as done at beginning of work, with color A for 3 rows, k 1 row color B, k 1 row color C, p 1 row color A.

MAIN SECTION: With larger needles, work in stockinette stitch for 2 rows with color A, then work Chart 2 for 10 rows, work 3 rows color A. Work Chart 1 for 6 rows (using alternate color scheme), work 2 rows color A, then purl back with color C, dec 3 sts evenly across row, to leave 88 (92–96) sts.

SHAPE TOP: Work with color C as follows: With right side facing, *k3 tog, k16 (17–18) sts, slip 1, k2 tog, pass slipped stitch over this st (psso),* repeat * to * 4 times—72 (76–80) sts. Purl back. Next row, *k3 tog, k12 (13–14) sts, slip 1, k2 tog, psso* 4 times—56 (60–64) sts. Purl back. Continue in this manner, dec 16 sts every right-side row, until no more decreases can be worked. With tapestry needle, weave end through remaining sts and draw tightly to close opening. Sew back seam using outside seam method described in Special Techniques chapter.

PINE TREE HAT CHARTS

Chart 1

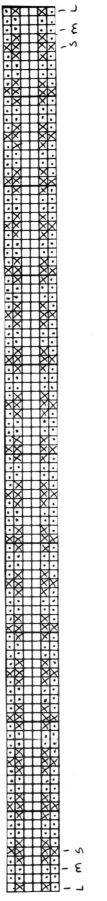

Chart 2

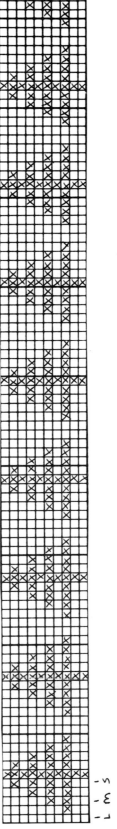

□ = A
X = B
· = C

29

Adult's Pine Tree Socks

These are heavy outdoor socks, good for cross-country skiing, etc.

SIZE: One size fits all

MATERIALS: One 100-gram (220-yard) skein Harrisville Two-Ply Tweed color Heath (A), one 100-gram (220-yard) skein each Harrisville Two-Ply no. 7 Sandalwood (B) and no. 31 Evergreen (C). One set each sizes 4 and 6 double-pointed needles, or size needed to obtain correct gauge.

GAUGE: In stockinette stitch, 5 sts = 1 inch.

Cable (worked in 6 sts):
Rows 1 & 2: P 2, k2, p2.
Row 3: P2, k next 2 sts together, leave on needle and k first stitch again, drop both sts off needle together, p2.
Rows 4, 5, and 6: As row 1.
Repeat these 6 rows for pattern.

LEFT SOCK, CUFF: With larger needles and color C, cast on 52 sts loosely. Divide sts evenly on smaller needles and place a marker at beginning of row. Work around in k2, p2 rib for 1 row with color C, then continue with color B until ribbing is 2½ inches long.

LEG: Change to larger needles. Then work with color A, inc 1 st at beg of row—53 sts. Divide sts by putting 14 sts on first needle, 15 sts on second needle, and 24 sts on third needle. Next row, work as follows: knit 29 sts, cable on 6 sts, knit 9 sts, cable on 6 sts, knit 3 sts. Work in established pattern for rest of leg. *At the same time,* at 4 inches from cuff, work first dec as follows: K2 tog, work to last 2 sts, ssk. Repeat this dec row once more 6 rounds later, to leave 49 sts. Work even until 5 (6–7) inches from cuff, or desired length. Divide sts as follows for heel: Place first 12 sts and last 11 sts on one needle for heel, and leave remaining 26 sts on holder for instep.

HEEL: Working on these 23 sts only, with color B, work as follows: Row 1 (wrong side): Sl first st, purl across. Row 2: Sl first st, k across. Repeat these 2 rows until you have 18 rows worked. Place marker on this row. **Turn heel as follows:** With wrong side facing, sl 1, p 13, p2 tog, p1, turn work. Sl 1, k6, ssk, k1, turn. Sl 1, p7, p2 tog, p1, turn. Sl 1, k8, ssk, k1, turn. Sl 1, p9, p2 tog, p1, turn. Continue in this manner, working toward sides of heel and having 1 st more between the decs on each row until 15 sts remain.

GUSSETS AND FOOT: With right side facing, and using color A, start in the center of the 15 heel sts and knit across last 7 sts from heel, pick up and k 10 sts on side of heel, work across 26 sts taken from instep holder, pick up and k 10 sts on side of heel, work across 8 remaining sts from heel. Place marker for beginning of row—you should have 17 sts on first needle, 26 sts on second needle, 18 sts on third needle (61 sts). K 1 round. Decrease round: K to within last 3 sts on first needle, k2 tog, k 1; k across sts on second needle; on third needle, k1, ssk, k to end of row. Repeat these last 2 rounds 5 times more—49 sts. Work evenly until foot length is 7 (8–9) inches from heel marker. Place 12 sts on first and third needles, 25 sts on second needle.

TOE: Work with color B. Round 1: K to within 3 sts from end of first needle, k2 tog, k1; on second needle, k1, ssk, k to within last 3 sts, k2 tog, k1; on third needle, k1, ssk, k to end. Round 2: K around. Repeat these 2 rounds 5 times more, then repeat round 1 every round until 13 sts remain. Close toe by weaving end sts together (see Special Techniques).

PINE TREE MOTIFS: With tapestry needle and color C, work duplicate stitch motifs shown in Chart in knitted band between cable patterns, following chart. Begin 2 rows below cuff and leave 4 rows between motifs. Work as many complete motifs as space will allow in the band. (See Special Techniques for instructions on duplicate stitch.)

RIGHT SOCK: Work as for left sock, positioning cables on first needle instead of last, thus reversing motif placement.

ADULT'S PINE TREE SOCKS CHART

Child's Pine Tree Socks

SIZES: Small (Medium–Large)

MATERIALS: One (100-gram, 440-yard) skein each Harrisville Shetland Style no. 40 Beige (A), no. 37 Henna (B), and no. 26 Peacock (C). One set size 2 double-pointed needles, or size needed to obtain correct gauge. One ring marker. Tapestry needle.

GAUGE: In stockinette stitch, 7 sts = 1 inch.

CUFF: With color A, loosely cast on 40 (44–48) sts. Work around in k1, p1 rib, being careful not to twist stitches on first row. Place ring marker at beginning of row. Work *2 rows color B and 2 rows color C* 2 times, then 2 rows color B. With color A, and repeating the 5 rows of Chart 1, knit every round until 3½ (4–4½) inches from beginning, or desired calf length.

CHILD'S PINE TREE SOCKS CHARTS

Chart 1   Chart 2

= A
= B
= C

HEEL: Place first and last 10 (10–12) sts on one needle for heel and leave remaining 20 (24–24) sts on holder for instep. With color C, work on these 20 (20–24) sts for 11 (11–13) rows, slipping first stitch of every row and ending when ready to work a right-side row. Place marker on this row.

TURN HEEL: Row 1: Sl 1, k 11 (11–14) sts, ssk, k1. Turn work, leaving remaining sts unworked. Row 2: Sl 1, p 6 (6–7), p2 tog, p1, turn. Row 3: Sl 1, k 6 (6–7), ssk, k1, turn.

Repeat rows two and three 4 (4–5) more times. Next row, sl 1, p6 (6–7), p2 tog, p0 (0–1), to leave 8 (8–10) sts remaining.

FOOT: With right side facing, resume working around with color A, following Chart 1. Work across 4 (4–5) sts from heel needle, place ring marker for beginning of row, work on remaining 4 (4–5) sts on needle, pick up and k 6 (6–7) sts on side of heel, work across 20 (24–24) sts taken from instep needle, pick up and k6 (6–7) sts on side of heel, work to marker—40 (44–48) sts. Continue knitting around until 5 (6–7) inches from heel marker, or desired foot length before toe. Move ring marker on next row by knitting 5 (5–6) sts at beginning of row and placing marker in this new location.

SHAPE TOE: Work with color C. Row 1: K7 (8–9), ssk, k2, k2 tog, k14 (16–18), ssk, k2, k2 tog, k7 (8–9), to leave 36 (40–44) sts. Row 2: K6 (7–8), ssk, k2, k2 tog, k12 (14–16), ssk, k2, k2 tog, k6 (7–8), to leave 32 (36–40) sts. Continue in this manner, dec 4 sts every row, until 8 sts remain. Pull end of yarn through remaining sts and draw tightly to close.

PINE TREE MOTIF: Following Chart 2, with tapestry needle and color C, work one motif on right side of leg for right sock, and on left side for left sock in duplicate stitch. (See Special Techniques for instructions on duplicate stitch.)

Child's Pine Tree Mittens

p. 18

SIZES: Small (Medium–Large)

MATERIALS: One 100-gram (440-yard) skein each Harrisville Shetland Style no. 40 Beige (A), no. 37 Henna (B), and no. 26 Peacock (C). One set size 2 needles, or size needed to obtain correct gauge. Tapestry needle. Two ring markers.

GAUGE: In stockinette stitch, 7 sts = 1 inch.

CUFF: With color A, loosely cast on 32 (36–40) sts. Work around in k1, p1 rib, being careful not to twist stitches on first row. Work 2 rows with color B and 2 rows with color C for 2 inches, inc 4 sts evenly in last row to give 36 (40–44) sts.

MITTEN: Knit around with color A following Chart 1 for rest of mitten, placing ring markers after first and before last stitch. At ¾ (1–1¼) inch from cuff, begin shaping thumb gore, knitting in established color pattern on hand stitches and with color A alone on thumb gore.

THUMB GORE: Inc 1 st by knitting in front and back of stitch before first marker and in stitch after last marker. Knit around next row. Work in this manner, increasing 6 (7–8) times for a total of 48 (54–60) sts. Leave these new 12 (14–16) sts on holder for thumb. On remaining 36 (40–44) sts, resume working with color A, following Chart 1 until 3½ (4½–5½) inches from ribbing, or desired length to top. Work 2 rows with color B.

TOP: Work with color C as follows: Row 1: *Ssk, k 14 (16–18), k2 tog* 2 times, to leave 32 (36–40) sts. Row 2: K around. Row 3: *Ssk, k12 (14–16) sts, k2 tog* 2 times—28 (32–36) sts. Row 4: K around. Work in this manner, dec 4 sts every row, until 20 (24–28) sts remain. Cut yarn. Weave end shut (see Special Techniques).

THUMB: With color A and following Chart 1, knit around on 12 (14–16) sts from thumb holder and pick up 2 sts where thumb meets the hand, for a total of 14 (16–18) sts. Work around with

color A for ¾ (1–1¼) inch. Next row, k 2 tog around—7 (8–9) sts. Next row, k1 (0–1), k2 tog around—4 (4–5) sts. Cut yarn. With tapestry needle, pass end of yarn through remaining sts and pull tightly to close.

PINE TREE MOTIF: With tapestry needle and color C, work one pine tree motif, following Chart 2 and using duplicate stitch, in center of top side of each mitten. (See Special Techniques for instructions on duplicate stitch.)

CHILD'S PINE TREE MITTENS CHARTS

Chart 1   Chart 2

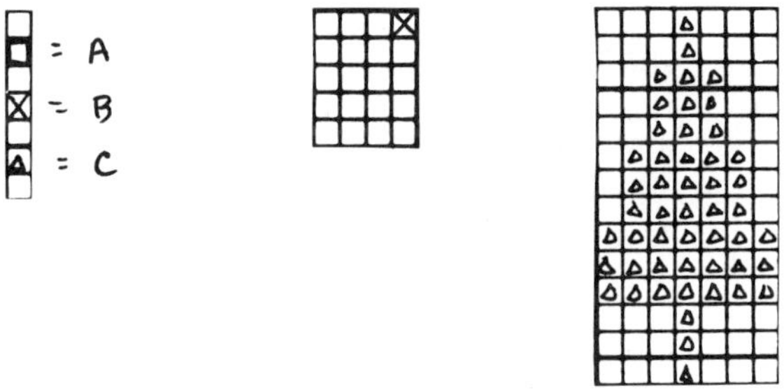

□ = A
☒ = B
△ = C

Child's Pine Tree Hat

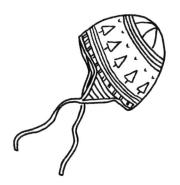

SIZES: 17 (18–19) inches in circumference

MATERIALS: One 100-gram (440-yard) skein each Harrisville Shetland Style no. 40 Beige (A), no. 37 Henna (B), and no. 26 Peacock (C). One pair size 2 needles, or size needed to obtain correct gauge. Two size 2 double-pointed needles. Tapestry needle.

GAUGE: In stockinette stitch, 7 sts = 1 inch.

RIBBED EDGE: With color A, cast on 119 (125–133) sts. Row 1: K1, *p1, k1. Row 2: P1, *k1, p1. Repeat these 2 rows for ¾ inch. Then, in stockinette stitch for rest of hat, work 2 rows with color B, 2 rows with color C, and 2 rows with color B. Work with color A for 4 rows, then follow chart, repeating last 5 rows until 4 (4½–5) inches from beginning. End ready to work a right-side row.

SHAPE TOP: Work 2 rows with color B, 2 rows with color C, and 2 rows with color B, then work with color A for rest of hat. *At the same time,* dec 11 (5–1) sts evenly across first row of color B—108 (120–132) sts. Purl back. Begin shaping. Row 1: *K2 tog, k10; rep from * across —99 (110–121) sts. Row 2 and all wrong-side rows: Purl. Row 5: *K2 tog, k9; rep from * across —90 (100–110) sts. Continue in this manner, working decrease row every right-side row, until 9 (10–11) sts remain. Cut yarn, leaving an 18-inch tail. With tapestry needle, insert tail of yarn through remaining sts and draw tightly to close top. Sew back seam using the outside seam method (see Special Techniques).

EAR FLAPS (make two): At 2 (2¼–2½) inches from back seam, using color C and with right side facing, pick up and k 17 (19–21) sts on ribbed edge of hat. With wrong side facing, purl back with color C, then continue in stockinette stitch for 2 rows each of colors A, B and C, repeating for rest of flap. At 1 (1¼–1½) inch dec 1 st at each end on every right-side row 6 (7–8) times—5 sts. Do not break yarn.

MAKE CORD: With last color used in earflap, using 2 double-pointed needles, knit on the 5 sts. Without turning work, slip sts back to right end of needle and knit again. Repeat until cord is 10 inches long. Cut yarn. With tapestry needle, insert tail of yarn through all sts and pull tightly to close. Weave in end.

EDGING: With color C and 2 double-pointed needles, cast on 4 sts. Knit 3 sts, sl 1, pick up and knit stitch on edge of hat, pass slipped stitch over this stitch (psso). Without turning work, slip sts back to right end of needle and knit across, picking up one more stitch on edge of hat and working psso. Begin this edge at one cord of earflap and work to the next cord. Repeat for both front and back edges, being careful to keep tension of edging loose.

CHILD'S PINE TREE HAT CHART

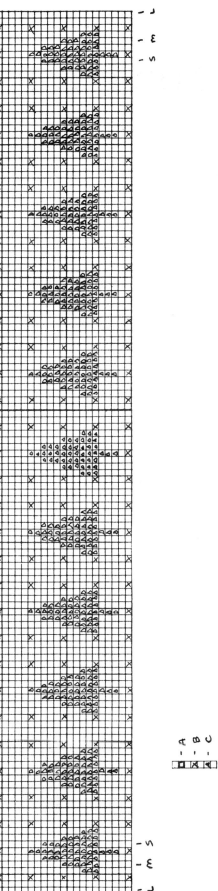

35

Long Deer Hat

SIZES: 18 (19–20) inches in circumference

MATERIALS: One 100-gram (440-yard) skein each Harrisville Shetland Style no. 41 Wedge-

wood (A), no. 34 Teak (B), and no. 16 Straw (C). One pair size 2 needles, or size needed to obtain correct gauge.

GAUGE: In stockinette stitch, 7 sts = 1 inch.

RIBBED EDGE: With color B, cast on 125 (133–139) sts. Row 1: K1, *p1, k1. Row 2: P1, *k1, p1. Repeat these 2 rows for 2 inches. Then, in stockinette stitch, follow chart, repeating last 12 rows (the "snowflake" pattern) until 5 (5½–6)

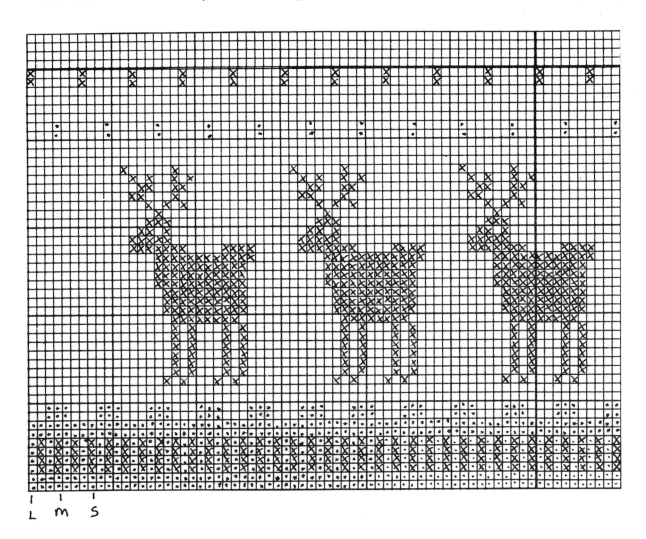

inches from beginning. End ready to work a right-side row, and dec 0 (0–1) st each end of last row —125 (133–137) sts.

SHAPE TOP: Keeping snowflake pattern as established, work decreases as follows: Row 1: K 29 (31–32) sts, k2 tog, ssk, k59 (63–65) sts, k2 tog, ssk, k 29 (31–32) sts, to leave 121 (129–133) sts. Row 2 and all wrong side rows: Purl. Row 3: K 28 (30–31) sts, k2 tog, ssk, k57 (61–63) sts, k2 tog, ssk, k28 (30–31) sts. Continue in this manner, dec 4 sts every other row until there are not enough sts left to work decreases. Cut yarn, leaving a 20-inch tail.

FINISHING: With tapestry needle, insert tail of yarn through remaining sts and draw tightly to close top. Sew back seam using outside seam method (see Special Techniques).

TASSEL: Cut several strands each color 7 inches long. Fold in half and wrap tightly with another strand of yarn at about ¾ inch below fold. Attach at tip of hat.

- A
- B
- C

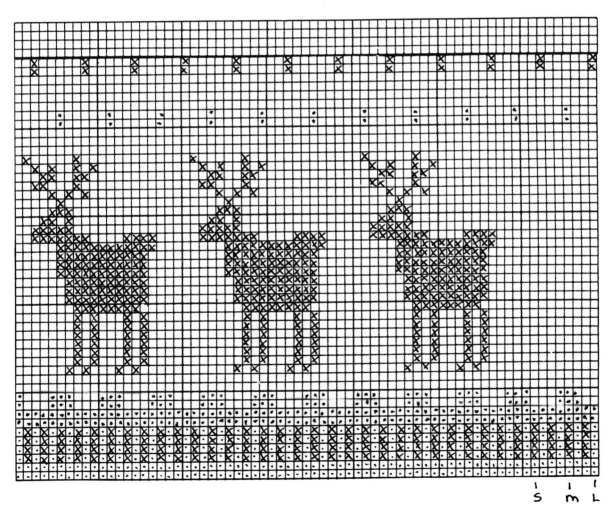

S   M   L

Square Deer Hat

MATERIALS: One 100-gram (440-yard) skein each Harrisville Shetland Style no. 4 Lichen (A), no. 56 Rose (B), and no. 32 Cocoa (C). One pair size 2 needles, or size needed to obtain correct gauge.

SIZES: 18 (19–20) inches in circumference

GAUGE: In stockinette stitch, 7 sts = 1 inch.

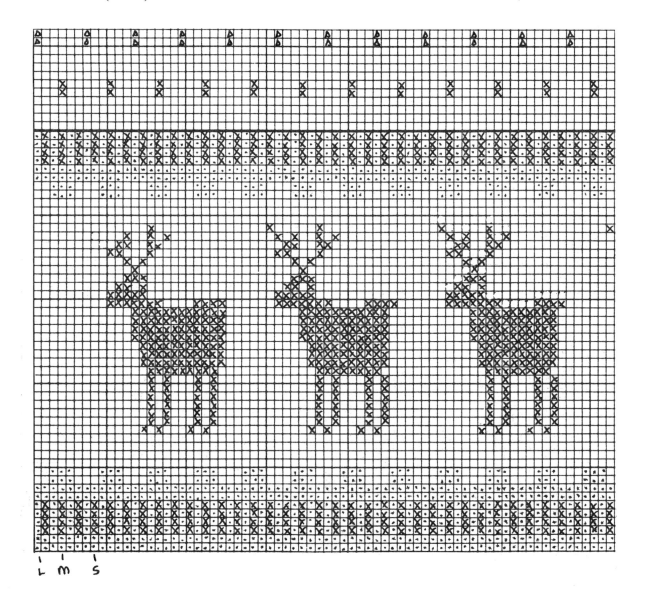

LINING: With color A, cast on 125 (133–139) sts very loosely. Work in stockinette stitch for 3 inches, ending ready to work a wrong-side row. Knit across.

HAT: Follow chart, repeating last 12 rows until 9 (10–11) inches from purled ridge row, evenly decreasing 1 (1–3) sts across last row to leave 124 (132–136) sts.

FINISHING: Place first 31 (33–34) sts on one needle, place next 62 (66–68) sts on another needle, and place last 31 (33–34) sts on same needle as first group of sts. With right sides together, join the 2 groups of sts using the knitted seam method (see Special Techniques chapter). Then sew each corner together. Fold hem to inside and stitch loosely in place, allowing for stretch. Turn hat right-side out.

- A
- B
- C

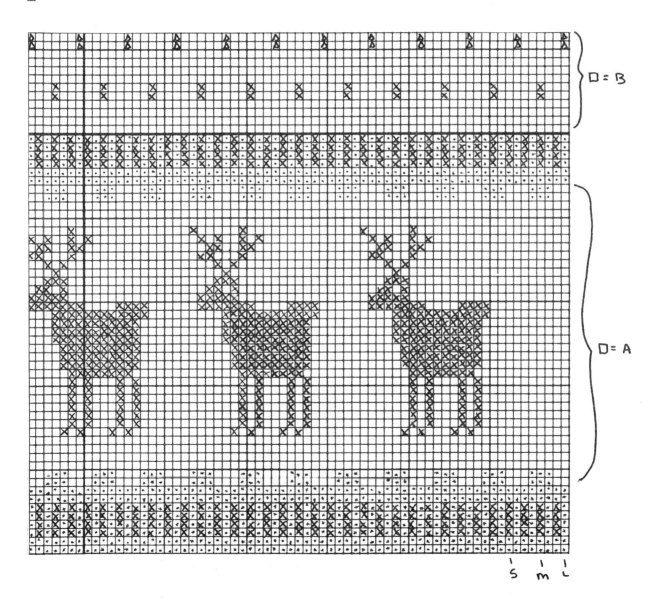

Deer Mittens

SIZES: Child's Small (Medium–Large); Adult's Small (Medium–Large)

MATERIALS: One 100-gram (440-yard) skein each Harrisville Shetland Style no. 4 Lichen (A), no. 56 Rose (B), and no. 32 Cocoa (C). One pair size 2 needles, or size needed to obtain correct gauge. Tapestry needle.

GAUGE: In stockinette stitch, 7 sts = 1 inch.

RIGHT MITTEN: With color B, cast on 55 (61–67); 67 (73–79) sts. Row 1: K1, *p1, k1. Row 2: P1, *k1, p1. Repeat both rows once. Then, work in stockinette stitch, following Chart 1, until 2 (2¼–2½); 2½ (2¾–3) inches from beginning, dec 18 (18–20); 18 (20–22) sts evenly in last row to leave 37 (43–47); 49 (53–57) sts.

With color B, work in k1, p1 rib for ½ (½–¾); ¾ (¾–1) inch. Next, work in stockinette stitch, following Chart 2, for 10 rows, then work even with color A to tip of mitten. *At the same time,* at 1¾ (2–2¼); 2½ (2¾–3) inches from wrist ribbing, knit across first 8 (9–10); 10 (11–12) sts and leave on holder for thumb, work to end of row. Next row, cast on 8 (9–10); 10 (11–12) sts over bound-off sts from previous row, then work to end of row. Continue working as established until 3½ (4½–5½); 6½ (7–7½) inches from wrist ribbing, decreasing 1 st and placing marker at center of last wrong-side row to leave 36 (42–46); 48 (52–56) sts.

SHAPE TOP with color B: Row 1: K1, k2 tog, work to within 3 sts before center marker, ssk, k1, slip marker, k1, k2 tog, work to last 3 sts, ssk, k1. Row 2: Purl. Repeat these 2 rows 4 more times. Weave end shut (see Special Techniques chapter).

THUMB: With color A, work across 8 (9–10); 10 (11–12) sts from thumb holder, and then pick up and k 8 (9–10); 10 (11–12) sts on bound-off edge—16 (18–20); 20 (22–24) sts. Work in stockinette stitch for ¾ (1–1¼) inch; 2¼ (2½–2¾) inches. With right side facing, k2 tog across entire row, leaving 8 (9–10); 10 (11–12) sts. Next row, p0 (1–0); p0 (1–0) st, p2 tog to end of row—4 (5–5); 5 (6–6) sts. Break yarn, weave end of yarn through these remaining sts, and pull tightly to close end.

LEFT MITTEN: Work same as right mitten, leaving sts on holder for thumb from end of row instead from beginning.

DEER MOTIF: With tapestry needle and color C, duplicate stitch deer motif from Chart 3, with deer facing right on left mitten and facing left on right mitten. (See Special Techniques chapter for instructions on duplicate stitch.)

FINISHING: Sew side seams using outside seam method (see Special Techniques chapter).

DEER MITTENS CHARTS

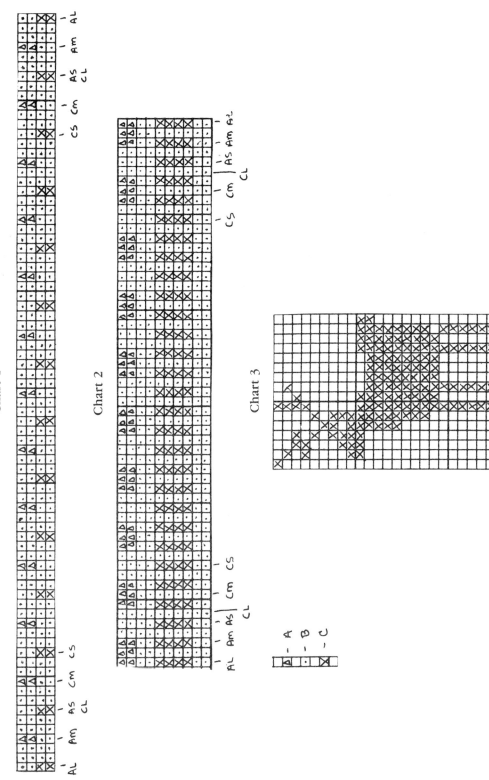

Chart 1

Chart 2

Chart 3

Deer Scarf

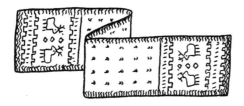

FINISHED SIZE: 8½ inches x 45 inches

MATERIALS: One skein each Harrisville Shetland Style no. 4 Lichen (A), no. 56 Rose (B), and no. 32 Cocoa (C). One pair size 2 needles, or size to obtain correct gauge. 2 bobbins.

GAUGE: In stockinette stitch, 7 sts = 1 inch.

Begin: With color A, cast on 59 sts. Work in garter stitch (k every row) for 1 inch. Then, continue in garter st on first and last 3 sts with color A, using bobbins. Work in stockinette stitch, following chart on center 53 sts, repeating the last 12 rows until approximately 38½ inches from beginning, or 6½ inches less than total desired length, ending with row 4 or 10 of this 12-row repeat. Then work following chart in reverse, from row 54 down to row 1, completing to match other end. Bind off all sts.

DEER SCARF CHART

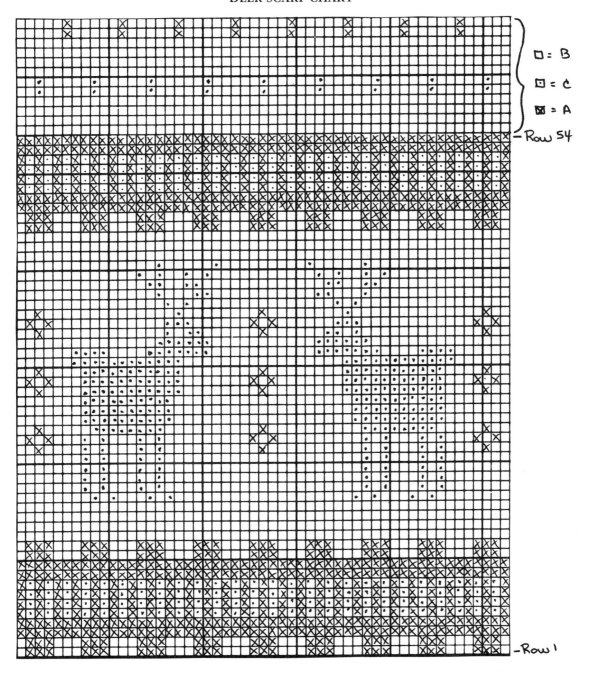

□ : B

⊡ : C

☒ : A

— Row 54

— Row 1

□ = A

☒ = B

· = C

Child's Deer Vest

SIZES: 2 (4–6). Finished chest, measurements 24 (26–28) inches

MATERIALS: One 100-gram (440-yard) skein each Harrisville Shetland Style no. 41 Wedgwood (A), no. 34 Teak (B), and no. 16 Straw (C). One pair each size 1 and 2 needles, or size needed to obtain correct gauge. One 16-inch size 1 circular needle. Tapestry needle. Four ⅜-inch buttons.

GAUGE: In stockinette stitch, 7 sts = 1 inch.

Note: Vest is worked in one piece to armhole.

Begin: With color A and smaller needles, cast on 147 (161–175) sts. Row 1: P1, *k1, p1. Row 2: K1, *p1, k1. Repeat these 2 rows for 1½ inches, inc 14 sts evenly in last row to give 161 (175–189) sts. Then, in stockinette stitch with larger needles, follow chart from Y to Z then back to Y every row, repeating last 12 rows for rest of piece. *At the same time,* at 7½ (8–8½) inches from beginning, divide for armholes.

RIGHT FRONT: With right side facing, work across 31 (35–38) sts and leave remaining sts on holder. Working on this side only, dec 1 st at armhole edge every other row 5 times. *At the same time,* at neck edge, begin shaping as follows: with right side facing, K1, ssk, work to end of row. Repeat this row every right-side row 9 (11–11) more times. When all shapings are completed, you should have 16 (18–21) sts left. Work even until 13 (14–15) inches from beginning. Leave sts on holder.

BACK: Bind off first 14 sts from holder and work on next 71 (77–85) sts for back, leave remaining sts on holder. To shape armholes, dec 1 st each end every other row 5 times—61 (67–75) sts. Work even in established pattern until back is same length as right front to shoulder. Leave sts on holder.

LEFT FRONT: Bind off first 14 sts from holder and work on remaining 31 (35–38) sts. Dec 1 st at armhole edge every other row 5 times. At neck edge, work to last 3 sts, k2 tog, k1, and repeat this decrease row every right-side row 9 (11–11) times more. Work even until same length as right front to shoulder. Leave sts on holder.

NECKBAND: Join shoulders using the knitted seam method (described in Special Techniques chapter) and leave remaining 29 (31–33) sts on holder for back of neck. Beginning at lower front edge of right side, with color A and smaller needles, pick up and k 47 (50–53) sts on edge of front to point where neck shaping begins. Pick up and k 37 (39–43) sts to shoulder seam, work across 29 (31–33) sts from back holder, pick up and k 37 (39–43) sts to point where neck shaping begins, 47 (50–53) sts to lower edge, for a total of 197 (209–225) sts. Work in reverse stockinette stitch (purl on right side, knit on wrong side). At ¼ inch from beginning, with right side facing for girl's version and wrong side facing for boy's version, work on 3 sts, *yo, work 2 sts tog, work on 12 (13–14) sts* 3 times, yo, work 2 sts tog, work to end of row. Work even for ½ inch and repeat buttonhole row again. Work even for ¼ inch more. Bind off all sts.

ARMHOLE BANDS: With circular needle and color A, begin at underarm and pick up and k 85 (91–97) sts. Work around, purling every row for 1½ inches. Bind off all sts.

FINISHING: Fold buttonhole band in half to inside. Align buttonholes and join together with buttonhole stitch, using tapestry needle and color B. Sew buttons opposite buttonholes. Fold arm-

CHILD'S DEER VEST CHART

hole bands in half to inside and stitch loosely in place, allowing for stretch. (See Special Techniques chapter for instructions on buttonhole stitch.)

Chickadee Hat

SIZES: 18 (19–20) inches in circumference

MATERIALS: One 100-gram (440-yard) skein each Harrisville Shetland Style no. 35 Chestnut (A), no. 20 White (B), no. 16 Straw (C), and no. 11 Black (D). One pair each sizes 1 and 2 needles, or size needed to obtain correct gauge.

GAUGE: In stockinette stitch, 7 sts = 1 inch.

BRIM: With color A and smaller needles, cast on 117 (123–129) sts loosely. Work in garter stitch (knit every row) for ¾ (1–1) inch. Inc 10 sts evenly in last row, ending ready to work a wrong-(right–right)-side row, giving 127 (133–139) sts.

HAT: With larger needles and in stockinette stitch, work 1 (2–4) rows with color A, then work 20 rows following Chart 1, then work 1 (2–4) rows with color A. Next, work Chart 2 for 17 rows, dec 23 (21–19) sts across last row, leaving 104 (112–120) sts.

SHAPE TOP: Row 1 (right side): Row 1: K10 (11–12) sts, *sl 1, k2 tog, psso, k3 tog, k20 (22–24) sts; work from * 3 times, sl 1, k2 tog, psso, k3 tog, k10 (11–12) sts. Row 2 and all wrong-side rows: Purl. Row 3: K8 (9–10) sts, *sl 1, k2 tog, psso, k3 tog, k16 (18–20) sts; work from * 3 times, sl 1, k2 tog, psso, k3 tog, k8 (9–10) sts. Continue in this manner, working decreases every right-side row until no more decreases can be made. Cut yarn, leaving a 15-inch tail. Weave tail through remaining sts and pull tightly to close opening, then sew back seam using outside seam method (see Special Techniques chapter).

Chickadee Mittens

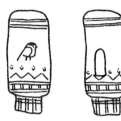

SIZES: Child's Small (Medium–Large); Adult's Small (Medium–Large)

MATERIALS: One 100-gram (440-yard) skein each Harrisville Shetland Style no. 35 Chestnut (A), no. 20 White (B), no. 16 Straw (C), and no. 11 Black (D). One pair size 2 needles, or size needed to obtain correct gauge. Tapestry needle.

GAUGE: In stockinette stitch, 7 sts = 1 inch.

RIGHT MITTEN: With color D, loosely cast on 37 (43–47); 49 (53–57) sts. Row 1: K1, *p1, k1. Row 2: P1, *k1, p1. Continue this ribbing, working the next 2 rows with color B, 2 more rows with color D, then work rest of cuff with color A. Work in ribs until cuff is 3 (3–3½); 3½ (3½–4) inches wide. Then work in stockinette stitch, following Chart 2. Continue with color A alone for remainder of mitten.

At the same time, at 1¾ (2–2¼); 2½ (2¾–3) inches from wrist ribbing, knit across first 8 (9–10); 10 (11–12) sts and leave on holder for thumb, work to end of row. Next row, cast on 8 (9–10); 10 (11–12) sts over bound-off sts from previous row, then work to end of row. Continue working until 3½ (4½–5½); 6 (6½–7) inches from wrist ribbing, decreasing 1 st and placing marker at center of last wrong-side row—36 (42–46); 48 (52–56) sts.

SHAPE TOP: K1, ssk, work to 3 sts before center marker, k2 tog, k1, slip marker, k1, ssk, work to last 3 sts, k2 tog, k1. Purl back. Work these 2 rows 5 times, working 2 rows with color D, 2 rows with color A, 2 rows with color D, then with color A for rest of mitten. Weave end shut (see Special Techniques chapter).

THUMB: With color A, work across 8 (9–10); 10 (11–12) sts from thumb holder, then pick up and k 8 (9–10); 10 (11–12) sts on bound-off edge, for a total of 16 (18–20); 20 (22–24) sts. Work in stockinette stitch for ¾ (1–1¼); 2¼ (2½–2¾) inches. Next right-side row, k2 tog around entire row—8 (9–10); 10 (11–12) sts. Last row, p0 (1–0); p0 (1–0) st, p2 tog to end of row—4 (5–5); 5 (6–6) sts. Break yarn and weave end of yarn through these remaining sts; pull tightly to close end.

LEFT MITTEN: Work same as right mitten, leaving sts on holder for thumb at end of row instead of at beginning.

CHICKADEE MOTIF: With tapestry needle and following motif on Chart 1, duplicate stitch chickadee pattern with bird facing right on left mitten and facing left on right mitten. (See Special Techniques chapter for duplicate stitch instructions.)

FINISHING: Sew side seams using outside seam method (see Special Techniques). Since the bottom half of the cuff will be worn folded back, the lower half of the cuff seam should be stitched toward the outside—to be hidden once the cuff is turned back.

CHICKADEE HAT AND MITTENS CHARTS

Chart 1

Chart 2

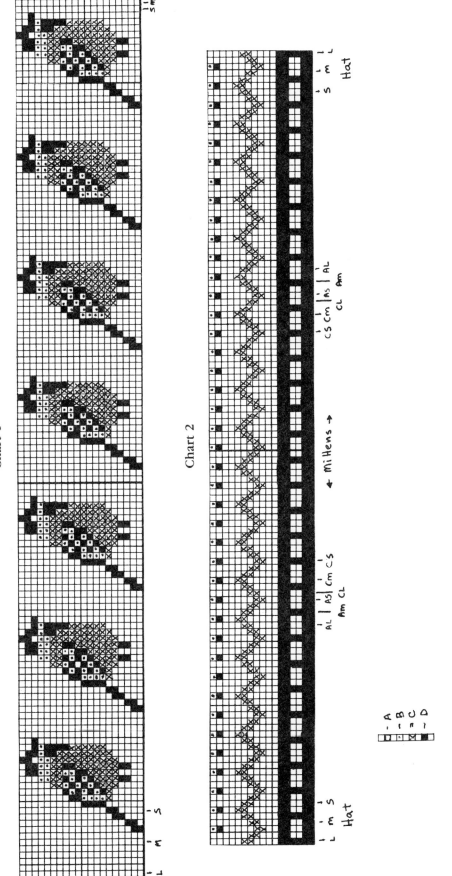

Country Geese Hat

SIZES: 18 (19–20) inches in circumference

MATERIALS: One 100-gram (220-yard) skein each Harrisville Two-Ply no. 20 White (A), no. 30 Hemlock (B) and no. 58 Aster (C). One pair size 6 needles, or size needed to obtain correct gauge.

GAUGE: In stockinette stitch, 5 sts = 1 inch.

CUFF: With color A, cast on 91 (95–101) sts. Row 1: K1, *p1, k1. Row 2: P1, *k1, p1. Repeat these 2 rows until 9 (13–15) rows are worked.

With wrong side facing, knit 1 row across. Continuing in stockinette stitch, work 1 (2–3) rows with color A, then work Chart 1 for 6 rows. With color A, work 1 (2–3) rows in stockinette stitch, then repeat rows 1 & 2 (ribbing) 1 (2–2) times. Work 2 rows in stockinette stitch in color A.

MAIN SECTION: Working in stockinette stitch for rest of hat, follow Chart 2 for 28 rows, evenly decreasing 7 (11–5) sts across last row to leave 84 (84–96) sts.

SHAPE TOP: Row 1: With color A, right side facing, *k5 (5–6) sts, k2 tog; repeat from * across —72 (72–84) sts. Row 2 and all wrong-side rows: Purl. Row 3: *k4 (4–5) sts, k2 tog; repeat from * across—60 (60–72) sts. Continue in this manner until 12 sts remain. Break yarn, leaving a 20-inch tail.

FINISHING: With tapestry needle, weave end through remaining sts and pull tightly to close opening. Sew back seam using outside seam method (see Special Techniques chapter). Fold ribbed cuff to inside and stitch in place, using loose tension to allow for stretch.

COUNTRY GEESE HAT CHARTS

Chart 1

Chart 2

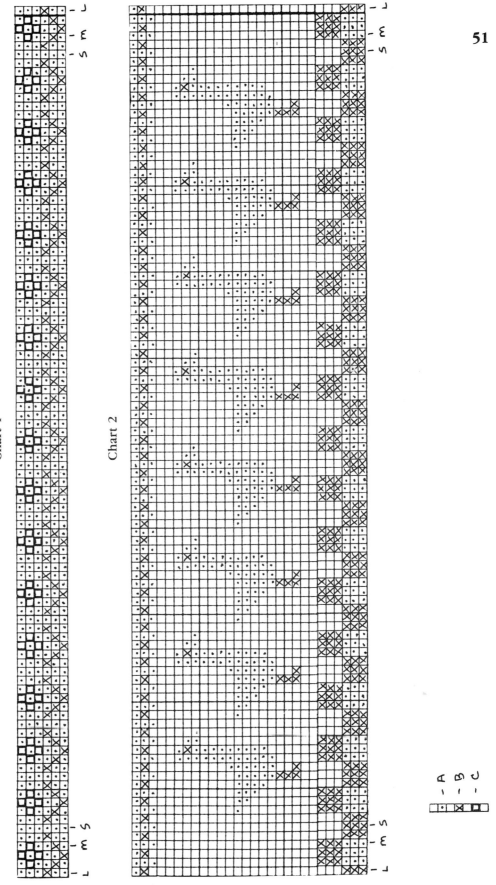

51

- A
- B
- C

Flock of Sheep Hat

SIZES: 18 (19–20) inches in circumference

MATERIALS: One 100-gram (220-yard) skein each Harrisville Two-Ply no. 36 Rust (A), no. 11 Black (B), no. 14 Gold (C), and no. 2 Pearl (D). One pair size 6 needles, or size needed to obtain correct gauge.

GAUGE: In stockinette stitch, 5 sts = 1 inch.

CUFF: With color A, cast on 91 (95–101) sts. Row 1: K1, *p1, k1. Row 2: P1, *k1, p1. Repeat these 2 rows for 1½ inches, ending ready to work a right-side row. With color B, knit 2 rows.

MAIN SECTION: Working in stockinette stitch for rest of hat, work 2 (3–4) rows with color A, work Chart 1 for 7 rows, work 1 (2–3) rows with color A, work Chart 2 for 13 rows, work 2 (3–4) rows with color A, work Chart 1 for 7 rows. Work 2 (3–2) rows with color A, evenly decreasing 3 (7–5) sts across last row to leave 88 (88–96) sts.

SHAPE TOP: Row 1: With color A, right side facing, k8 (8–9) sts, *sl 1, k2 tog, psso, k3 tog, k16 (16–18) sts; repeat from * 3 times, then end with k8 (8–9) sts—72 (72–80) sts. Row 2 and all wrong-side rows: Purl. Row 3: K6 (6–7) sts, *sl 1, k2 tog, psso, k3 tog, k12 (12–14) sts; repeat from * 3 times, then end with k6 (6–7) sts—56 (56–64) sts. Continue in this manner until no more decreases can be worked. Break yarn, leaving a 20-inch tail.

FINISHING: With tapestry needle, weave end through remaining sts and pull tightly to close opening. Sew back seam using outside seam method (see Special Techniques chapter). Fold ribbed cuff in half to inside and stitch in place, using loose tension to allow for stretch.

FLOCK OF SHEEP HAT CHARTS

Chart 1

Chart 2

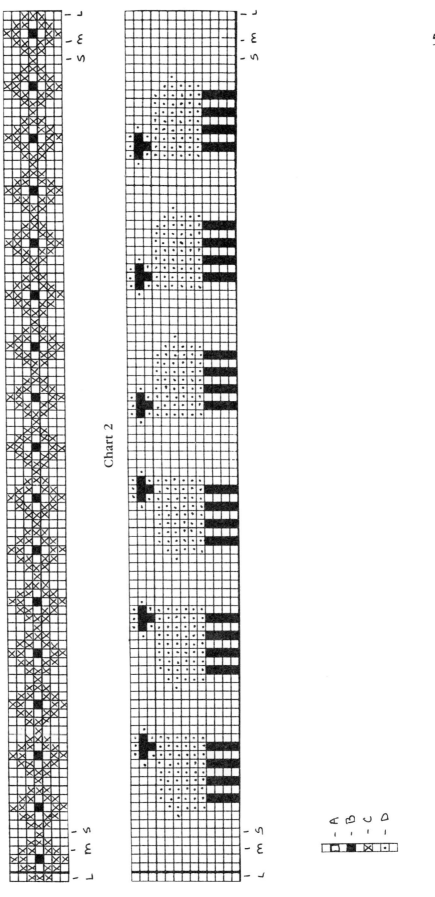

Child's Bunny Hat

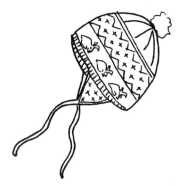

SIZES: 17 (18–19) inches in circumference

MATERIALS: One 100-gram (220-yard) skein Harrisville Two-Ply no. 44 Cobalt (A), no. 18 Camel (B), no. 20 white (C), and no. 54 Garnet (D). One pair size 6 needles, or size needed to obtain correct gauge. One size F crochet hook.

GAUGE: In stockinette stitch, 5 sts = 1 inch.

MAIN SECTION: With color A, cast on 85 (91–95) sts. In stockinette stitch, work 4 (4–6) rows with color A, then follow Chart 1 for 8 rows. Work 2 (4–6) rows with color A, then work Chart 2 for 19 rows. Next, work 1 (3–5) rows with color D, decreasing 1 (7–11) sts evenly across last row to leave 84 sts.

SHAPE TOP: Row 1: With color D, right side facing, *k5, k2 tog; repeat from * across—72 sts. Row 2 and all wrong-side rows: Purl. Row 3: *K4, k2 tog; repeat from * across—60 sts. Continue in this manner until 12 sts remain. Break yarn leaving a 15-inch tail. With tapestry needle, weave end through remaining sts and pull tightly to close opening. Leave yarn end free for now.

EARFLAPS: Measure 2 (2¼–2½) inches from back edge, and with color C, pick up and knit 15 (17–19) sts, inserting needle on ridge formed by purled sts on first row of wrong side of work. Work shaping and color placement following Chart 3. Break yarn.

RIBBED BRIM: With crochet hook and color D, work 75 (81–85) single crochet sts on lower edge of hat. Fasten off. With right side facing and color D, pick up and k 75 (81–85) sts, inserting needle in each single-crochet stitch along edge. Row 1: P1, *k1, p1. Row 2: K1, *p1, k1. Bind off all sts loosely.

CROCHETED TIES: With crochet hook and color D, work in single crochet along one side of earflap, ch 41, work in slip stitch back up this chain, work in single crochet along other side of earflap. Fasten off.

FINISHING: With yarn end left free, sew back seam using outside seam method (see Special Techniques chapter).

Using a mix of all 4 colors, make a 2-inch diameter pompom (see Special Techniques chapter) and attach to top of hat.

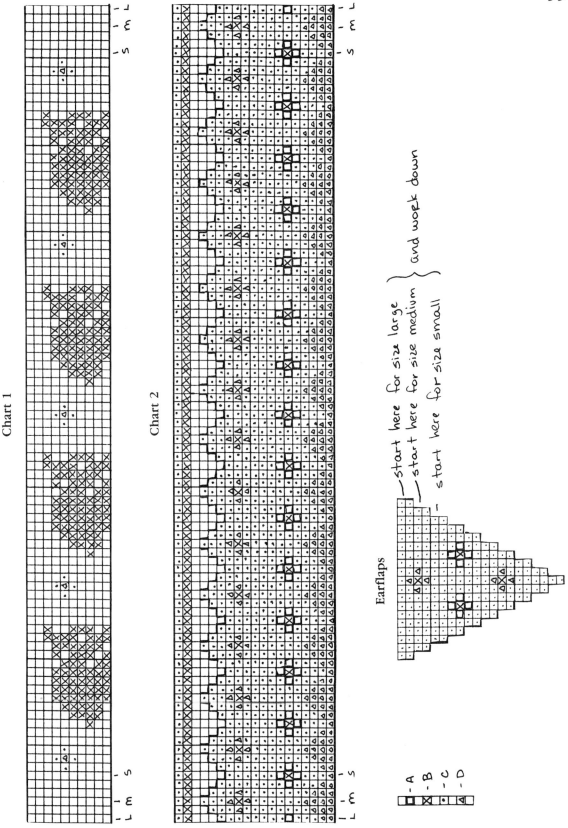

CHILD'S BUNNY HAT CHARTS

Chart 1

Chart 2

Earflaps

start here for size large
start here for size medium } and work down
start here for size small

☐ - A
◻X◻ - B
· - C
◁ - D

Summer Cottage Hat

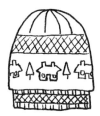

SIZE: 18 (19–20) inches in circumference

MATERIALS: One 100-gram (220-yard) skein Harrisville Two-Ply no. 31 Evergreen (A), one 100-gram skein each Harrisville Two-Ply Tweed True Blue (B), and Adobe (C). One pair size 6 needles, or size needed to obtain correct gauge.

GAUGE: In stockinette stitch, 5 sts = 1 inch.

CUFF: With color A, cast on 91 (95–101) sts. Row 1: K1, *p1, k1. Row 2: P1, *k1, p1. Repeat row 1. With wrong side facing, knit across. Work rows 5 to 8 of Chart 1. With color A, knit 2 rows, then repeat rows 1 and 2 (ribbing) 2 times. With right side facing, knit across with color A.

MAIN SECTION: In stockinette stitch for rest of hat, work 2 (4–4) rows with color C, work Chart 2 for 13 rows, work 3 (3–5) rows with color C, work Chart 1 for 8 (12–16) rows, decreasing 0 (4–10) sts evenly across last row to leave 91 sts.

SHAPE TOP: Row 1: With color A and right side facing, *k5, k2 tog; repeat from * across—78 sts. Row 2 and all wrong-side rows: Purl. Row 3: *K4, k2 tog; repeat from * across—65 sts. Continue in this manner until 13 sts remain. Break yarn leaving a 15-inch tail.

FINISHING: With tapestry needle, weave end through remaining sts and pull tightly to close opening. Sew back seam using outside seam method (see Special Techniques chapter).

SUMMER COTTAGE HAT CHARTS

Chart 1

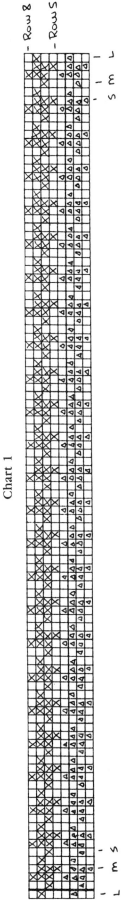

Chart 2

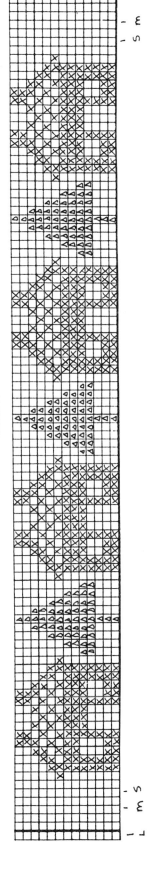

57

Crayon Kids Pullover

SIZES: 2 (4–6–8). Finished chest measurements 26 (28–30–32) inches

MATERIALS: Harrisville Two-Ply: 2 (2–3–3) 100-gram (220-yard) skeins no. 57 Red (A), 1 (1–1–2) 100-gram skeins no. 20 White (B), one 100-gram skein each of no. 26 Peacock (C), no. 44 Cobalt (D), and no. 15 Daisy (E). One pair each sizes 5 and 6 needles, or size needed to obtain correct gauge. One 16-inch size 5 circular needle.

GAUGE: In stockinette stitch with larger needles, 5 sts = 1 inch.

BACK: With smaller needles and color A, cast on 61 (67–71–77) sts. Row 1: K1, *p1, k1. Row 2: P1, *k1, p1. Work in this manner for 2 inches, inc 4 sts evenly across last row to give 65 (71–75–81) sts. Then, with larger needles, work Chart 1 in stockinette stitch, repeating the last 14 rows and alternating "snowflake" colors B, C, D, and E for rest of back.

SHAPE NECK: At 14 (15–16–17) inches from beginning, with right side facing, work across 24 (26–28–30) sts and leave remaining sts on holder. On this side only, dec 1 st at neck edge every other row 2 times. Work as established on remaining 22 (24–26–28) sts until 15 (16–17–18) inches from beginning. Leave sts on holder. To complete other side, leave center 17 (19–19–21) sts on holder for back of neck; work on remaining sts as for first side.

FRONT: Work as for back until 13 (14–15–16) inches from beginning. With right side facing, work across 27 (29–31–33) sts and leave remaining sts on holder. On this side only, dec 1 st at neck edge every other row 5 times. Work as established on remaining 22 (24–26–28) sts until 15 (16–17–18) inches from beginning. Leave sts on holder. To complete other side, leave center 11 (13–13–15) sts on holder for front of neck; work on remaining sts as for first side.

SLEEVES: With smaller needles and color A, cast on 33 (35–37–39) sts. Work in ribbing as for lower back for 2 inches, inc 8 (8–10–10) sts evenly across last row to give 41 (43–47–49) sts. Then, with larger needles, work Chart 2 in stockinette stitch, repeating the last 14 rows and alternating "snowflake" colors for rest of sleeve. *At the same time,* inc 1 st at each end every inch 7 (9–9–11) times, for a total of 55 (61–65–71) sts. Work even until 11 (12–13–14) inches from beginning or total desired length. Bind off all sts.

NECKBAND: Join shoulders using the "knitted seam" method (described in Special Techniques chapter). With circular needle and color A, beginning at left shoulder seam, pick up and k 11 sts on left side of neck, work across 11 (13–13–15) sts from front holder, pick up and k 16 sts on right side of neck, work across 17 (19–19–21) sts from back holder, pick up and k 5 sts on back side of neck—60 (64–64–68) sts. Work around in k1, p1 rib for 1 inch. Using larger needle, bind off loosely in rib stitch.

FINISHING: Measure 6 (6½–7–7½) inches on each side of shoulder seams and place markers on armhole edge. Set in sleeves between markers, stretching slightly to fit. Sew underarm and side seams below sleeves using outside seam method (see Special Techniques chapter).

CRAYON KIDS PULLOVER CHARTS
Chart 1

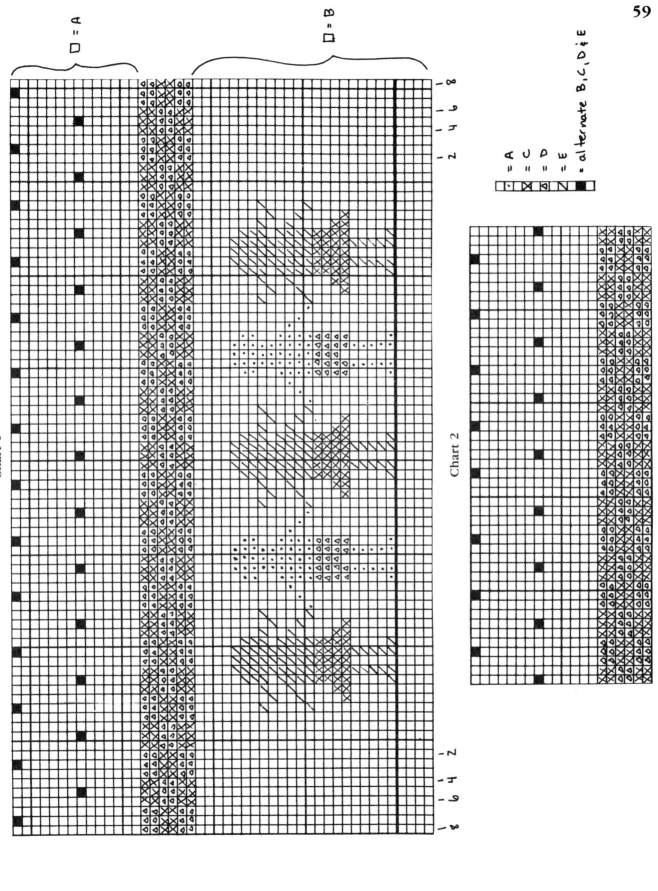

Chart 2

Crayon Kids Hat

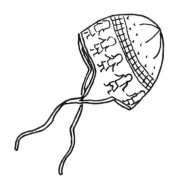

SIZES: 17 (18–19) inches

MATERIALS: One 100-gram (220-yard) skein each Harrisville Two-Ply no. 57 Red (A), no. 20 White (B), no. 26 Peacock (C), no. 44 Cobalt (D), and no. 15 Daisy (E). One pair size 6 needles, or size needed to obtain correct gauge. One size E crochet hook.

GAUGE: In stockinette stitch with larger needles, 5 sts = 1 inch.

EARFLAPS (MAKE 2): With color A, cast on 5 sts. Work even in stockinette st for 2 rows, inc 1 st each end of next row, then every other row 3 (4–5) more times for a total of 13 (15–17) sts. Leave sts on holder.

BRIM: With color B, cast on 9 (10–11) sts. With right side facing, work across the 13 (15–17) sts from first earflap, cast on 41 (41–39) sts, work across the 13 (15–17) sts from second earflap, cast on 9 (10–11) sts for a total of 85 (91–95) sts. Work chart in stockinette stitch, repeating last 14 rows for rest of hat or until 5½ (6–6½) inches from cast-on row, dec 1 (1–5) sts evenly across last row—84 (90–90) sts.

SHAPE TOP: With color A and right side facing, *K2 tog, k4; repeat from * across—70 (75–75) sts. Row 2 and all wrong-side rows: Purl. Row 3: *K2 tog, k3; repeat from * across—56 (60–60) sts. Continue in this manner until 14 (15–15) sts remain. Cut yarn, leaving a 15-inch tail. Thread through remaining sts and pull tightly to close opening. Sew back seam using outside seam method (see Special Techniques chapter).

CROCHETED EDGING AND TIES: With crochet hook and color A, begin at back seam, working in single crochet around back edge of hat to tip of earflap. Work a chain 10 inches long, work in slip stitch back up this chain for first tie and continue in single crochet on other side of earflap. On front edge, work around second earflap as for first one, then on back edge ending at back seam. Fasten off.

CRAYON KIDS HAT CHART

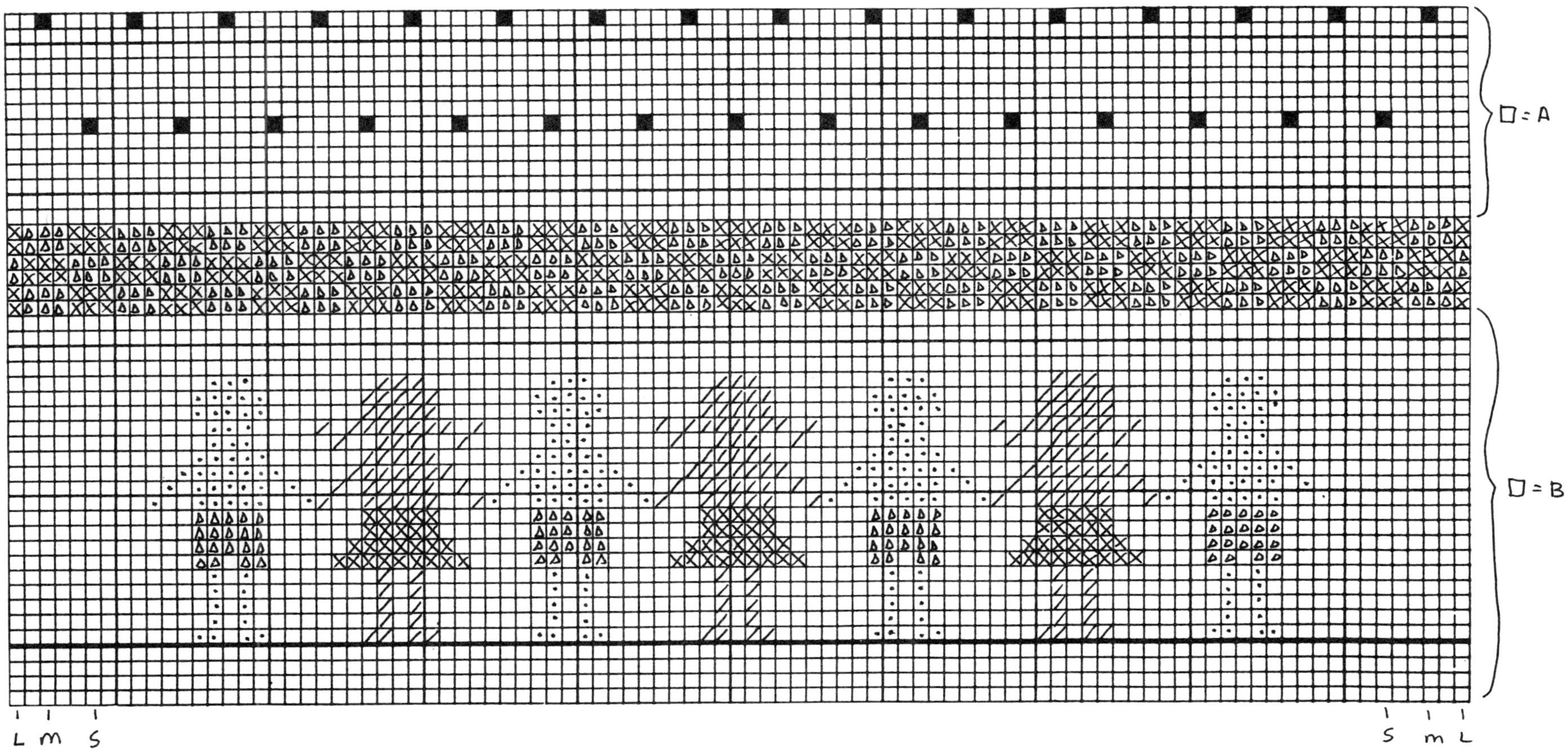

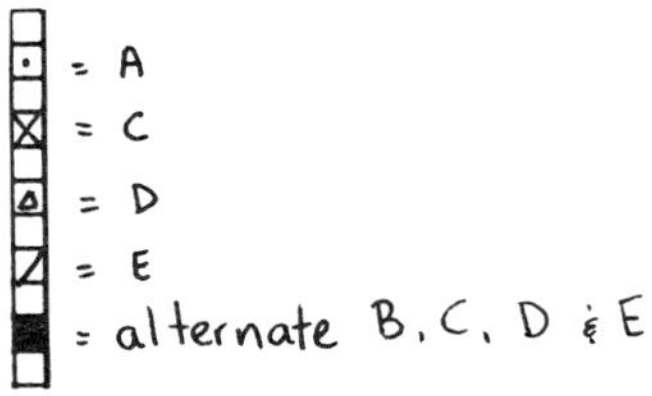

□ = A

□ = B

61

· = A
⊠ = C
◢ = D
╱ = E
■ = alternate B, C, D & E

Crayon Kids Mittens p. 19

SIZE: Children's small (Medium–Large)

MATERIALS: One 100-gram (220-yard) skein each Harrisville Two-Ply no. 57 Red (A), no. 20 White (B), no. 26 Peacock (C), no. 44 Cobalt (D), and no. 15 Daisy (E). One pair each sizes 5 and 6 needles, or size needed to obtain correct gauge. One tapestry needle.

GAUGE: In stockinette stitch with larger needles, 5 sts = 1 inch.

CUFF: With color A and larger needles, cast on 27 (31–35) sts. With smaller needles and color B, work as follows: Row 1: K1, *p1, k1. Row 2: P1, *k1, p1. Repeat these 2 rows until 2 inches from beginning.

HAND: With larger needles, work chart in stockinette stitch, repeating last 10 rows for rest of hand. *At the same time,* at ¾ (1–1¼) inch above ribbing, begin shaping thumb gore.

THUMB GORE: Row 1 (right side): Inc in first stitch by knitting in front and back of it, knit to last 2 sts, inc in next stitch, k1. Row 2 and all wrong-side rows: Purl. Row 3: K1, inc in next st, knit to last 3 sts, inc in next st, k2. Row 5: K2, inc in next st, knit to last 4 sts, inc in next st, k3. Continue in this manner until you have 39 (45–51) sts on needle. Next row, leave first and last 6 (7–8) sts on holders for thumb. Continue working around on remaining 27 (31–35) sts until 3½ (4½–5½) inches from cuff. In center of last wrong-side row, dec 1 st and place marker—26 (30–34) sts.

SHAPE TOP: Row 1: With color A, ssk, work to 2 sts before marker, k2 tog, slip marker, ssk, work to last 2 sts, k2 tog. Row 2: Purl. Repeat these 2 rows 3 more times, to leave 10 (14–18) sts. Cut yarn and weave end shut (see Special Techniques chapter).

THUMB: With color B, work across 6 (7–8) sts from first holder, then across 6 (7–8) sts from second holder—12 (14–16) sts. Work in stockinette stitch on these sts until ¾ (1–1¼) inch from beginning, ending ready to work a right-side row. Next row, k2 tog across—6 (7–8) sts. With wrong side facing, p0 (1–0), p2 tog across—3 (4–4) sts. Cut yarn and thread end through remaining sts. Pull tightly to close tip.

FINISHING: Sew side of hand and thumb to end of cuff.

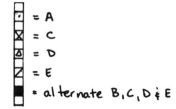

= A
= C
= D
= E
= alternate B, C, D & E

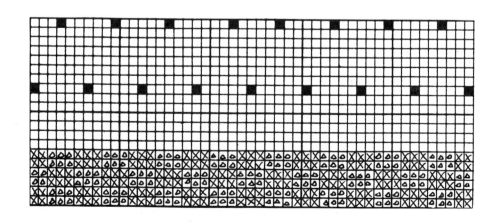

Pine Tree Christmas Stocking

LENGTH: Approximately 17½ inches

MATERIALS: One 100-gram (220-yard) skein each Harrisville Two-Ply no. 20 White (A), no. 30 Hemlock (B), and one 100-gram skein Harrisville Two-Ply Tweed Burgundy (C). One pair size 6 needles, or size needed to obtain correct gauge. One size E crochet hook.

GAUGE: In stockinette stitch, 5 sts = 1 inch.

Note: This stocking is worked back and forth on 2 needles from the cuff down.

CUFF AND LEG: With color C, cast on 61 sts. Row 1: K1, *p1, k1. Row 2: P1, *k1, p1. Repeat these 2 rows with color C for 1¼ inches. Then with right side facing and working in stockinette stitch, work rows 1 through 56 of chart. Next row, with right side facing, work across with color A.

HEEL: Row 1: With wrong side facing and color C, purl across 15 sts and leave remaining sts on holder, turn. Row 2: Slip first st, knit to end of row. Repeat these 2 rows 5 more times—12 rows. Begin working short rows as follows: P2, p2 tog, p1, turn; sl 1, k3, turn; p3, p2 tog, p1, turn; sl 1, k4, turn; p4, p2 tog, p1, turn; sl 1, k5, turn; p5, p2 tog, p1, turn; sl 1, k6, turn; p6, p2 tog, p1, turn; sl 1, k7, turn; p7, p2 tog, p1, turn —9 sts remain. Break yarn and leave sts on holder.

Leave center 31 sts of work on holder for instep and work on remaining 15 sts as follows: Row 1: With right side facing and color C, work across. Row 2: Slip first st, purl to end of row. Repeat these 2 rows 5 more times—12 rows. Begin working short rows as follows: K2, k2 tog, k1, turn; sl 1, p3, turn; k3, k2 tog, k1, turn; sl 1, p4, turn; k4, k2 tog, k1, turn; sl 1, p5, turn; k5, k2 tog, k1, turn; sl 1, p6, turn; k6, k2 tog, k1, turn; sl 1, p7, turn; k7, k2 tog, k1, turn—9 sts remain. Break yarn.

INSTEP AND GUSSETS: Starting at beginning of a right-side row, follow rows 28 to 17 of chart, then rows 7 to 16, then rows 6 to 1. Work across 9 sts from right half of heel, pick up and k 6 sts on side of heel, work across 31 sts from instep, pick up and k 6 sts on side of heel, work across 9 sts from left half of heel, for a total of 61 sts. Purl back.

Next, work shaping as follows, keeping color pattern as consistent as possible throughout decreases:
Row 1 (right side): K14, k2 tog, k29, ssk, k14, leaving 59 sts.
Row 2 and all wrong-side rows: Purl.
Row 3: K13, k2 tog, k29, ssk, k13, to leave 57 sts.
Row 5: K12, k2 tog, k29, ssk, k12, to leave 55 sts.
Row 7: K11, k2 tog, k29, ssk, k11, to leave 53 sts.
Row 9: K10, k2 tog, k29, ssk, k10, to leave 51 sts.
Row 11: K9, k2 tog, k29, ssk, k9, to leave 49 sts.
Continue working as established on these remaining 49 sts, following chart rows indicated previously and decreasing 1 st on last row (row 1 of chart)—48 sts.

TOE: Row 1 (right side): With color C, k9, k2 tog, k2, ssk, k18, k2 tog, ssk, k9, to leave 44 sts. Row 2 and all wrong-side rows: Purl. Row 3: K8, k2 tog, k2, ssk, k16, k2 tog, k2, ssk, k8, to leave 40 sts. Continue in this manner, dec 4 sts every right-side row, until 16 sts remain. Leave sts unbound.

FINISHING: Right-side out, fold toe so that seam meets in the center under the foot, and weave toe shut. Sew back seam. (See Special Techniques chapter for instruction on weaving and sewing seams.)

LOOP: With crochet hook and color C, ch 16. Inserting hook in second chain, work in slip stitch across. Break yarn. Fold loop in half and attach at top of stocking.

PINE TREE CHRISTMAS STOCKING CHART

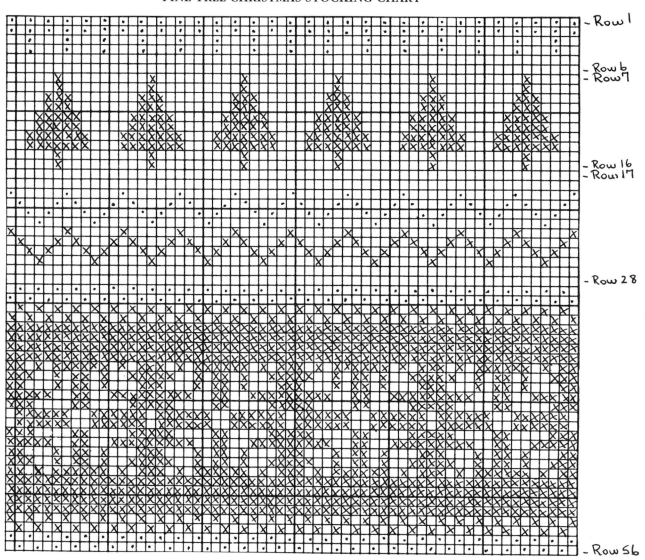

- □ - A
- ⊠ - B
- · - C

Norwegian Christmas Stocking

LENGTH: Approximately 18 inches

MATERIALS: One 100-gram (220-yard) skein each Harrisville Two-Ply no. 20 White (A), no. 31 Evergreen (B), and no. 57 red (C). One pair size 6 needles, or size needed to obtain correct gauge. One size E crochet hook. One tapestry needle.

GAUGE: In stockinette stitch, 5 sts = 1 inch.

Note: Stocking is worked back and forth on 2 needles from the cuff down. In main part of stocking color C is worked in duplicate stitch once knitting is complete.

CUFF AND LEG: With color C, cast on 65 sts. Row 1: K1 color C, *p2 color B, k2 color C. Row 2: *P2 color C, k2 color B; repeat from *, end with p1 in color C. Repeat these 2 rows 2 more times. Then, right-side facing and working in stockinette stitch, work rows 1 to 23 of chart. Repeat rows 16 to 23 for rest of stocking.

At 10 inches from beginning, ending ready to work a wrong-side row, mark next row on chart and work heel as follows: Row 1: With color C, purl across 16 sts and leave remaining sts on holder, turn. Row 2: Slip first st, knit to end of row. Repeat these 2 rows 5 more times—12 rows. Begin working short rows as follows: P2, p2 tog, p1, turn; sl 1, k3, turn; p3, p2 tog, p1, turn; sl 1, k4, turn; p4, p2 tog, p1, turn; sl 1, k5, turn; p5, p2 tog, p1, turn; sl 1, k6, turn; p6, p2 tog, p1, turn; sl 1, k7, turn; p7, p2 tog, p1, turn—10 sts remain. Break yarn and leave sts on holder.

Leave center 33 sts of work on holder for instep and work on remaining 16 sts as follows: Row 1: Right side facing, with color C, knit across. Row 2: Slip first st, purl to end of row, Repeat these 2 rows 5 more times—12 rows. Begin working short rows as follows: K2, k2 tog, k1, turn; sl 1, p3, turn; k3, k2 tog, k1, turn; sl 1, p4, turn; k4,

k2 tog, k1, turn; sl 1, p5, turn; k5, k2 tog, k1, turn; sl 1, p6, turn; k6, k2 tog, k1, turn; sl 1, p7, turn; k7, k2 tog, k1, turn—10 sts remain. Break yarn.

INSTEP AND GUSSETS: At beginning of a right-side row, resume color work on marked row on chart. Work across 10 sts from right half of heel, with appropriate colors, pick up and k 6 sts on side of heel, work across 33 sts from instep, pick up and k 6 sts on side of heel, work across 10 sts from left half of heel—65 sts. Purl back in color pattern. Then, begin shaping as follows, keeping color pattern as consistent as possible throughout decreases: Row 1 (right side): K15, k2 tog, k31, ssk, k15, leaving 63 sts. Row 2 and all wrong-side rows: Purl. Row 3: K14, k2 tog, k31, ssk, k14, to leave 61 sts. Continue in this manner until 49 sts remain. Work as established on these sts (following chart) until 7 inches from tip of heel, decreasing 1 st on last row—48 sts.

TOE: Row 1 (right side): With color C, k9, k2 tog, k2, ssk, k18, k2 tog, k2, ssk, k9, to leave 44 sts. Row 2 and all wrong-side rows: Purl. Row 3: K8, k2 tog, k2, ssk, k16, k2 tog, k2, ssk, k8, to leave 40 sts. Continue in this manner, dec 4 sts every right-sided row until 16 sts remain. Leave sts unbound.

FINISHING: With tapestry needle, work a duplicate stitch with color C in places indicated on chart on main part of stocking. With right side out, fold toe so that seam meets in the center under the foot and weave toe shut. Sew back seam. (See Special Techniques chapter for instructions on sewing seams, duplicate stitch, and weaving seams.)

LOOP: With crochet hook and color C, ch 16. Inserting hook in second chain, work in slip stitch across. Break yarn. Fold loop in half and attach at top of stocking.

NORWEGIAN CHRISTMAS STOCKING CHART

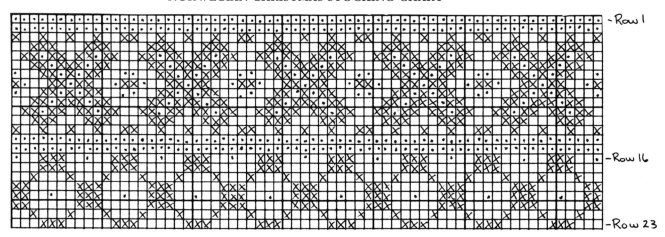

- □ - A
- ⊠ - B
- · - C

Leather-Soled Slippers

SIZES: Extra small (Small, Medium, Large, Extra large). These sizes will fit toddlers to adults.

MATERIALS: One 100-gram (220-yard) skein each Harrisville Two-Ply Tweed Wildflower (A), Burgundy (B), and Turquoise (C). One pair size 6 needles, or size needed to obtain correct gauge. One tapestry needle. One pair purchased fleece-lined leather soles of appropriate size.

GAUGE: In stockinette stitch, 5 sts = 1 inch.

CUFF: With color A, cast on 33 (37–41–45–49) sts. Row 1: K1, *p1, k1. Row 2: P1, *k1, p1. Repeat these 2 rows until 1½ (1½–2–2–2) inches from beginning.

LEG: Work in stockinette stitch, following Chart 1 for 19 rows.

HEEL: Row 1: With wrong side facing and color A, p8 (9–10–11–12) sts, leave remaining sts on holder. Row 2: Sl 1, knit to end of row. Repeat these 2 rows 3 (3–4–4–5) more times. Bind off all sts. To work other side, with wrong side facing, slip center 17 (19–21–23–25) sts on holder for instep, sl 1, p to end of row. Work on these 8 (9–10–11–12) sts as for first side of heel. Bind off all sts.

INSTEP: With right side facing and following Chart 2, pick up and k 8 (9–10–11–12) sts on side of right half of heel, work across 17 (19–21–23–25) sts from holder, pick up and k 8 (9–10–11–12) sts on side of left half of heel, for a total of 33 (37–41–45–49) sts. Purl back. Row 1: K6 (7–8–9–10) sts, k2 tog, place marker, k17 (19–21–23–25) sts, place marker, ssk, k6 (7–8–9–10) sts. Row 2: Purl. Row 3: K to 2 sts before first marker, k2 tog, slip marker, k to second marker, slip marker, ssk, k to end of row. Repeat these last 2 rows until 19 (21–23–25–27) sts remain. Work as established on these sts until 2 (2–2½–3–3) inches less than length of purchased leather sole.

SHAPE TIP: Row 1 (right side): Ssk, work to last 2 sts, k2 tog. Row 2: Purl. Repeat these 2 rows until 5 (7–7–9–9) sts remain. Bind off all sts.

FINISHING: Sew back seam using outside seam method (see Special Techniques chapter). With tapestry needle and color B, attach knitted section to leather sole in a criss-cross stitching pattern.

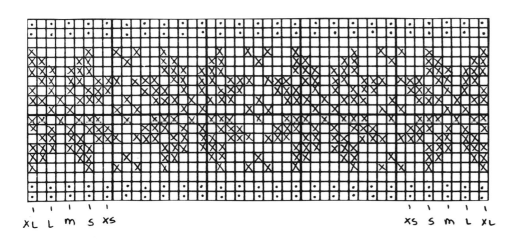
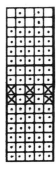

⬜ = A
⬛ = B
☒ = C

XL L M S XS

XS S M L XL

Knitted-Sole Slippers

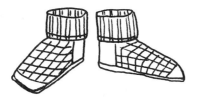

SIZES: Extra small (Small, Medium, Large, Extra large). Sole Length: 5 (6½ –8–9½ –11) inches

MATERIALS: One 100-gram (220-yard) skein Harrisville Two-Ply Tweed True Blue (A), one 100-gram skein each Harrisville Two-Ply no. 14 Gold (B), and no. 2 Pearl (C). One pair size 6 needles, or size needed to obtain correct gauge. One tapestry needle.

GAUGE: In stockinette stitch, 5 sts = 1 inch.

SOLE: Using 2 strands of wool together, cast on 8 (8–10–10–10) sts. Work in garter stitch (knit every row) for 6 rows. Inc 1 st each end of next row—10 (10–12–12–12) sts. Work for 12 rows. Inc 1 st each side of next row—12 (12–14–14–14) sts. Work even until 4 ½ (6–7½ –9–10½) inches from beginning.

SHAPE TIP: Dec 1 st each end of every row 4 times—4 (4–6–6–6) sts. Bind off all sts.

CUFF: With color A and single strand of wool, cast on 33 (37–41–45–49) sts. Work 2 rows with color B, then work the rest of cuff with color C: Row 1: K1, *p1, k1. Row 2: P1, *k1, p1. Repeat these 2 rows until 3 (3½–4–4–4) inches from beginning. With right side facing, knit across with color C.

HEEL TABS: Row 1: With wrong side facing and color B, p8 (9–10–11–12) sts, leave remaining sts on holder. Row 2: Sl 1, knit to end of row. Repeat these 2 rows 3 (3–4–4–5) more times. Bind off all sts. To work other side, with wrong side facing, slip center 17 (19–21–23–25) sts on holder for instep, sl 1, p to end of row. Work on these 8 (9–10–11–12) sts as for first side of heel. Bind off all sts.

INSTEP: With right side facing and color A, pick up and k 8 (9–10–11–12) sts on side of right half of heel, work across 17 (19–21–23–25) sts from holder, pick up and k 8 (9–10–11–12) sts on side of left half of heel, for a total of 33 (37–41–45–49) sts. Purl back. Follow chart for rest of foot, keeping colors as consistent as possible. Work as follows: Row 1: K6 (7–8–9–10) sts, k2 tog, place marker, k17 (19–21–23–25) sts, place marker, ssk, k6 (7–8–9–10) sts. Row 2: Purl. Row 3: K to 2 sts before first marker, k2 tog, slip marker, k to second marker, slip marker, ssk, k to end of row. Repeat these last 2 rows until 19 (21–23–25–27) sts remain. Work as established on these sts in color pattern until 4 ½ (5–7½ –9–10½) inches from back edge of heel tabs.

SHAPE TIP: Row 1 (right side): With color A, k1, slip 1, k2 tog, psso, work to last 4 sts, k3 tog, k1. Row 2: Purl. With color B for rest of toe, repeat these 2 rows 3 (3–3–4–4) more times, to leave 3 (5–7–5–7) sts. bind off all sts.

FINISHING: Sew back seam using outside seam method (see Special Techniques chapter). Since the upper half of the cuff will be worn folded down, the upper half of the cuff seam should be stitched toward the outside—to be hidden once the cuff is turned down. Attach top portion of slipper to sole.

KNITTED-SOLE SLIPPERS CHART

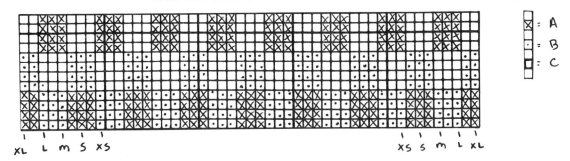

State of Maine Afghan

FINISHED MEASUREMENTS: 48 inches x 60 inches

MATERIALS: Harrisville Two-Ply (100-gram, 220-yard skeins): 5 skeins no. 4 Lichen (A), 2 skeins no. 20 White (B), 3 skeins no. 37 Henna (C), 2 skeins no. 31 Evergreen (D), and 2 skeins no. 11 Black (E). One each size 4 and 6 24-inch circular needles, or size needed to obtain correct gauge. Bobbins.

GAUGE: In stockinette stitch with larger needle and in color pattern, 5 sts = 1 inch.

MAIN PORTION: With size 4 needle and color E, cast on 239 sts. Working in garter stitch, work 2 rows even. Next row: k1, ssk, work to last 3 sts at end of row, k2 tog, k1. Wrong-side row: P2, k to last 2 sts, p2. Repeat shaping at the beginning and end of the next 7 right-side rows—223 sts. *At the same time,* work 2 more rows in garter stitch with color E (6 rows total). Then, with size 6 needles and in stockinette stitch, work 10 rows with color C, then 2 rows with color B.

Continuing with size 6 needles and in stockinette stitch, begin with row 3 of Chart 1 and work through to end of Chart 1. Work 6 rows with color A, then work across as follows for next 21 rows: Work 7 sts with color A, *work puffin from Chart 2 on 11 sts, work with color A on 11 sts; repeat from *, ending last repeat with color A on 7 sts. Once puffin band is completed, work 5 rows with color A.

Next, work 18 rows of Chart 1, then 6 rows with color A. Work across as follows for next 21 rows: Work 7 sts with color A, *work pine tree from Chart 3 on 11 sts; repeat from *, ending last repeat with color A on 7 sts. Once pine tree band is completed, work 5 rows with color A.

Next, work 18 rows of Chart 1, then 6 rows with color A. Work across as follows for next 21 rows: color A for 12 sts, then *work sailboat from Chart 4 on 19 sts, color A on 11 sts; repeat from *, ending last repeat with color A on 12 sts. Once sailboat band is completed, work 5 rows with color A.

Continue in this manner, alternating Chart 1 with Charts 2, 3, and 4, until approximately 58¼ inches from beginning, ending ready to work row 17 of Chart 1. With right side facing and with color B, k1, increase in next stitch by knitting in front and in back of it, work to last 3 sts, increase in next st, work to end of row. Purl back. Work 10 rows with color C, making increases as established at beginning and end of every right-side row. Then, with size 4 needle and color E, work in garter stitch, continuing increases until 239 sts are obtained. When 6 rows of garter stitch have been worked with color E, bind off all sts.

SIDE BORDER: On side edge of afghan, with size 6 needle and color B, pick up and k 283 sts. Purl back. With color C and in stockinette stitch work 10 rows, inc 1 st each end of every right-side row as instructed earlier. Then, with size 4 needle and color E, work in garter stitch for 6 rows, continuing increases as established, for a total of 299 sts. Bind off all sts. Work second side in the same manner.

FINISHING: Sew diagonal corners. Weave in all ends. Use tapestry needle and French knots to work puffin's eyes with color E. With damp cloth, steam press lightly to block. (See Special Techniques chapter for instructions on sewing seams and making French knots.)

STATE OF MAINE AFGHAN CHARTS

Chart 1

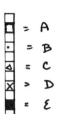

□ = A
· = B
△ = C
⊠ = D
■ = E

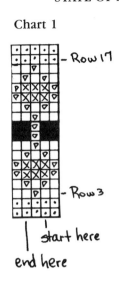

– Row 17

– Row 3

start here

end here

Chart 2

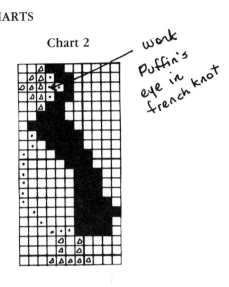

work Puffin's eye in french knot

Chart 3

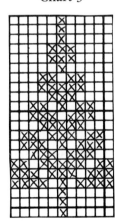

Chart 4

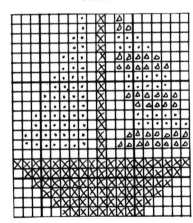

State of Maine Pillow

FINISHED MEASUREMENTS: 14 inches x 14 inches

MATERIALS: One 100-gram (220-yard) skein each Harrisville Two-Ply no. 4 Lichen (A), no. 20 White (B), no. 37 Henna (C), no. 31 Evergreen (D), and no. 11 Black (E). One pair size 6 needles, or size needed to obtain correct gauge. One 14-inch fiberfill pillow form. One piece of fabric 15 inches x 15 inches for back.

GAUGE: In stockinette stitch with larger needle and in color pattern, 5 sts = 1 inch.

Note: Pillow is formed by joining 4 triangular pieces together.

MAIN PIECES: With color E, cast on 71 sts and knit 2 rows even. Begin shaping sides as follows: Row 1: K1, ssk, work to last 2 sts, k2 tog, k1. Row 2: Purl. Row 3: As Row 1. Row 4: P1, p2 tog, purl to last 3 sts, p2 tog through back, p1.

Repeat these 4 rows for rest of triangle. *At the same time,* work color pattern as follows: After the first 2 rows, work 2 more rows with color E in garter stitch. Continuing in stockinette stitch for rest of pillow, work 4 rows with color C, 2 rows with color B, 6 rows with color A. Next row, place pine tree motifs from chart as follows: Work on 10 sts with color A (amount of sts after side edge decrease); work chart on next 11 sts; color A on 7 sts; chart on 11 sts; color A to end of row. Continue in this manner until chart is complete. Work 6 rows with color A, 2 rows with color B, 4 rows with color C. Next row, with color E, k1, sl 1, k2 tog, psso, k1. With color E, purl across 3 remaining sts. Leave on holder.

Work 3 more triangles in same manner.

ASSEMBLY: With tapestry needle, thread one end of color E yarn through the 12 sts remaining on holders (3 from each triangle), and draw tightly to close circle. Then sew each seam down to corner using outside seam method (see Special Techniques chapter).

FINISHING: Weave in all ends. With warm iron and damp cloth, block piece to size. With right sides together, sew knitted front to fabric back on three sides, leaving the fourth side open. Insert pillow form through opening. With needle and thread, close opening.

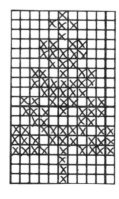